Political Grace

Political Grace
The Revolutionary Theology of John Calvin

Roland Boer

WESTMINSTER
JOHN KNOX PRESS
LOUISVILLE · KENTUCKY

© 2009 Roland Boer

1st edition
Published by Westminster John Knox Press
Louisville, Kentucky

09 10 11 12 13 14 15 16 17 18—10 9 8 7 6 5 4 3 2 1

All rights reserved. No part of this book may be reproduced or transmitted in any form or by any means, electronic or mechanical, including photocopying, recording, or by any information storage or retrieval system, without permission in writing from the publisher. For information, address Westminster John Knox Press, 100 Witherspoon Street, Louisville, Kentucky 40202-1396. Or contact us online at www.wjkbooks.com.

Scripture quotations, unless otherwise indicated, are from the New Revised Standard Version of the Bible, copyright © 1989 by the Division of Christian Education of the National Council of the Churches of Christ in the U.S.A., and are used by permission.

Scripture quotations marked RSV are from the Revised Standard Version of the Bible, copyright © 1946, 1952, 1971, and 1973 by the Division of Christian Education of the National Council of the Churches of Christ in the U.S.A., and are used by permission.

Excerpt from *Institutes of the Christian Religion,* trans. F. L. Battles, The Library of Christian Classics (1960; repr., Louisville, KY: Westminster John Knox, 2006). Used by permission of Westminster John Knox Press and SCM Press. All rights reserved.

Book design by Drew Stevens
Cover design by Eric Walljasper, Minneapolis, MN

Library of Congress Cataloging-in-Publication Data

Boer, Roland
  Political grace : the revolutionary theology of John Calvin / Roland Boer.
    p. cm.
  Includes bibliographical references (p.   ) and indexes.
  ISBN 978-0-664-23393-8 (alk. paper)
  1. Calvin, Jean, 1509–1564—Political and social views. 2. Christianity and politics—Reformed Church. 3. Liberty—Religious aspects—Reformed Church. 4. Grace (Theology) 5. Calvin, Jean, 1509–1564. Institutio Christianae religionis. I. Title.
  BX9418.B66 2009
  230'.42092—dc22
                                                           2009001812

PRINTED IN THE UNITED STATES OF AMERICA

∞ The paper used in this publication meets the minimum requirements
of the American National Standard for Information Sciences—
Permanence of Paper for Printed Library Materials, ANSI Z39.48-1992

Westminster John Knox Press advocates the responsible use of our natural resources.
The text paper of this book is made from 30% post-consumer waste.

For my father, Henk Boer

The brawling art which bears the name of speculative theology . . .
(*OS* 3:22.7–8)

The theologian's task is not to divert the ears with chatter, but to strengthen consciences by teaching things true, sure, and profitable.
(*Inst.* 1.14.4; *OS* 3:157.11–13)

Contents

Preface	ix
Introduction	xv
Argument	xv
Context	xviii
Sentence Production	xxiv
1. Protesting Too Much	**1**
Exegesis	2
Context	6
Theology	18
2. Bible: The Irrepressible Book	**21**
Out of the Reach of Human Hands	22
The Chicken and the Egg, Auto-Faith, God and the Holy Spirit	24
Conservatives and Radicals on the High Ground	32
3. Grace: The Question of Revolution	**39**
Letting Grace Have Its Head	39
Roping Grace Back In	48
The Revolutionary Paradox	55
4. Freedom: The Liberty of the Gospel	**57**
Curtailing Freedom	59
Private and Public	64
The Paradox of Calvinist Legalism	70
5. Politics: Overthrowing Ungodly Rulers	**75**
From Separation to Entanglement	76
Between Anarchy and Tyranny	78
What to Do with an Ungodly Ruler	80
Subject Only in the Lord	88

6. Paul: Inheriting an Insight — 93
Inheriting an Insight — 94
Calvin and Paul in Context — 104

Conclusion: What If? Calvin and the Spirit of Revolution — 111
Summary — 111
Bible — 116
Grace — 122
Freedom — 125
Politics — 129

Bibliography — 133

Scripture Index — 141

Subject Index — 143

Preface

This book is both deeply personal and strongly political. As any reader who makes some headway into the book will soon see (if it is not obvious from the table of contents), it is an "intervention" in the good old sense of the term. That is, it seeks to shake up some assumptions about Calvin—that he was purely an archconservative, that his thought provides the ideological underpinning for capitalism, that he makes sense of the recent neoconservatives (especially in the United States), that he is in favor of reform and not revolution, that he is responsible for a brutal and unforgiving theological system. Instead I argue that Calvin struggled deeply with the radical and reactionary elements of the Bible and his theological system. And I do so above all through a close reading of his *Institutes of the Christian Religion*.

But the book also reflects my own coming to terms with Calvin. The man's ideas and legacy run in my veins and capillaries. The practices of everyday life that seem to be inseparable from a Reformed commitment are still deeply ingrained. Even though I can now recognize them for what they are, it is all too easy to slip back into the assumption that they are a natural fit with the way the world operates. It might be the hesitation before going to a shop to buy some bread on a Sunday; the fact that I rarely watch television, especially on Sundays; the tension between getting a little bit more writing done and knowing that I really should take a regular break at least one day of the week—in short, the daily manifestations of that tension between a radical emphasis on grace and the deep tendency for Calvinism to become legalistic, the tension between the reliance on God alone and the propensity for moralizing and telling others what they should be doing.

My mother and father emigrated separately from the Netherlands and arrived in Australia in the late 1950s, when the Australian government offered free passage along with a heavy dose of propaganda about the place (most of it blatantly wrong). They came to Australia as Dutch Calvinists, unlike approximately 50 percent of Dutch immigrants who were Roman Catholic and joined the existing Roman Catholic structures.

More specifically, my parents came from the Gereformeerde Kerken in the Netherlands—the breakaway group from the Hervormde Kerk (I mention only the larger groups and not the myriad splinter groups). The reason: the old Reformed Church had slipped in its faithful Reformed witness. So it was time to return to that witness, which was really the true witness of the New Testament, or so they believed. In Australia, the immigrants of my parents' ilk formed the Reformed Churches of Australia, for they felt the need to carry on the true Reformed heritage in a new land. That is the context in which I grew up.

I remember a life that revolved around the church (my father was a minister): long services with either a long sermon or a long prayer or both; the training at sitting still as a young child through it all; church picnics; church quarrels; grace before and after meals whether in rain, hail, blizzard, shine, heat wave—whether in private or in public; Bible readings after the evening meal, before which we were not allowed to leave the table; a race off afterwards to read the passages that my father would censor; a request for forgiveness for all our sins in every possible prayer; Dutch spoken everywhere, so much so that I was in the situation of having a first language that was not the one of the country in which I was born.

It is well-nigh impossible to brush off such a heritage, although try I did in every possible manner. But it keeps coming back, so I decided it was best to come to terms with Calvin. I do not mean a cordial but frosty acquaintance—like Voltaire's habit of tipping his hat when passing a church so as to keep on good terms with the God he was rejecting. What I mean is that I would like to invite Calvin in for a couple of beers and a long talk on the balcony. I would like to get to know him and his thought much, much better. My guess is that it will take more than one long talk and that we will need to frequent my local watering hole for some time to come.

For some strange reason, a few years ago I bought the *Institutes of the Christian Religion*. Then I found a cheap collection of his biblical commentaries—the whole lot! They were translated and published by the Calvin Translation Society in the mid-nineteenth century. I even managed to track down a copy of the *Institutes* in Latin. Before I knew it, I was thinking a lot about Calvin. At first they were stray thoughts. Why did he die so early, at fifty-two? The answer seemed obvious: he worked himself to death. One comment brought this home to me like no other. It comes from the "Epistle to the Reader" prefaced to the last edition of the *Institutes*. Calvin mentions that he suffered from a form of malaria, which he calls the quartan fever (*febre quartana*), through the preceding winter while preparing the final edition ("final" largely because he died before any more could be completed). Did he slow down so that he might recover? Did he take some bed rest and get a decent night's sleep? No, he worked even harder: "The more the disease pressed upon me the less I spared myself, until I could leave a book behind me" (LCC 1:3; *OS* 3:5.19). It reminds me of the man who, when running out of gasoline in his car, would speed up in order to get to the service station before he ran out of fuel.

Calvin wrote so much in so short a time—and all of it by hand. Many would begin to mutter about the Protestant work ethic, how bad it is for you and so on, but it seems to me that Calvin suffered from another affliction: a demanding muse. Søren Kierkegaard had it and died as a result at forty-two. Karl Marx's muse made the same demands, and Marx managed to struggle on to sixty-two, even though he was riddled with ill health for most of it and ceased effective work by his early fifties. This muse demands that one write, no matter what the circumstances. Neither a sensitive nor alcoholic muse, this one expects writing no matter what. If you put anything in the way, such as a nonwriting job, hobbies, other people, or relationships, then they will suffer, as will your health and sleep. It is not for nothing that we find the following epigraph in the *Institutes*. It is drawn from Augustine: "I count myself one of the number of those who by profiting write and by writing profit" (*Epist*. V.ii., quoted in *OS* 3:7.8–9).

I asked many other questions as I read. Why did Calvin's system of thought seem so compellingly watertight? What did he see in Augustine, the highly skilled writer and church's theological hit man? Why does he write so well? Why is the *Institutes of the Christian Religion* so thick? And why did it become more and more obvious to me that in some way Calvin and Marx had a lot in common? Why indeed is there a distinct path from Calvin to Marx rather than a high fence? To answer these and other questions, I had to write a book.

This book, then, is a return to Calvin, although a rather different Calvin than many would expect. I should say a word on translations and citations. Following convention, *Inst* refers to the *Institutes of the Christian Religion*, and references are given in terms of book, chapter, and paragraph numbers. The only variation on this practice is when I refer to the English translations of Calvin's prefaces, both the epistle "to the reader" and the "Prefatory Address to the King Francis I of France"; in these cases I refer to *The Library of Christian Classics* in terms of volume and page number. As for the Latin original, I have made use of *Opera Selecta*, a five-volume selection of Calvin's work in Latin. The third, fourth, and fifth volumes contain the 1559 Latin edition of *Institutiones Christianae religionis*, edited by P. Barth and G. Niesel and published in 1957. The format for references is to cite *OS*, followed by volume, page, and line numbers. By and large I have followed the translation of the *Institutes* by Ford Lewis Battles in *The Library of Christian Classics* (1960, reissued 2006), although I have also checked it against Henry Beveridge's translation of 1845. I would like to acknowledge the permission to use Battles's translation by both Westminster John Knox Press and SCM Press. However, since Battles's translation is a little prosaic and misses some of the literary beauty of Calvin's Latin, I have at times offered my own translation. I have indicated where this is the case.

There is one further matter I would like to get out of the way. It really should not have to be mentioned in this day and age: lest I be accused of "eisegesis," of seeing my own image reflected in Calvin, I would remind any reader that there is no objective, unbiased reading. Indeed, the claim to be objective is itself highly suspicious for what it conceals. Unfortunately this point needs to be reasserted again and again, since I keep coming across one dolt after another who has been trained in some antediluvian institution where they still kid themselves that objectivity is possible.

A few words of thanks are in order. The idea that this book might be possible belongs to Philip Law, when he was still with Westminster John Knox Press. I still recall the way his eyes lit up when I mentioned I had been pondering a study of Calvin. The first chance to present some ideas from the book was provided by a kind invitation to give the Otago Lecture in Auckland in July 2008. Many thanks to James Harding, who dared to suggest I give the lecture, and to the Department of Theology and Religious Studies at Otago University for bravely agreeing with him. An invaluable conversation partner through it all has been Christina. She has had to endure my saying more than once, "May I read you a sentence from Calvin?" Mostly she has agreed, but not without a question.

I have dedicated this book to my father. We disagree with virtually every word the other says, and yet we meet frequently to renew the arguments once again. He has always insisted that the great achievements of trade unions in the Netherlands were inspired not by socialism but by Reformed tradition. I am not sure I agree, but this book is an effort to see if there is a radical element that may be found in Calvin. When I was well underway with writing this book, he was diagnosed with cancer. Despite ongoing treatment, I am very pleased to say that we continue our arguments, and I am sure he will disagree with every word I have written here. I only hope he gets a chance to read it.

I wrote the book over a few intense and focused months, from Easter 2008 until a crossing of the Tasman Sea in July of that year. Unlike the interminably verbose Calvin, who claimed rather incredibly, "I am striving for brevity" (*Inst.* 2.3.2; *OS* 3:273.8–9) and "by nature I love brevity" (*Inst.* 3.6.1; *OS* 4:147.5–6), I will keep this intervention short although perhaps not so sweet.

On the ship *Hansa Rendsburg,*
somewhere on the Tasman Sea
between Tauranga and Melbourne
July 2008

Introduction

The argument of this book may be summed up in one sentence: John Calvin let the radical *political* cat peek out of the *theological* bag only to try his hardest to push it back in and tie the bag up again.

ARGUMENT

Let me see if I can spin this idea out a little. The more I read Calvin's texts, the more it becomes clear to me that a major feature of his thought is a tension between the radical possibilities of his theological system and the effort to restrain those possibilities in light of his innate conservatism. It is as though he keeps on catching a glimpse of that radical theological and political potential only to take fright and backtrack.

In this book I focus on specific moments of that tension.[1] In particular, I am interested in the implication of a high doctrine of Scripture, the centrality of grace, the freedom of the gospel, and the treatment of "civil order" in the final chapter of the *Institutes*. I deal with the Bible first. Over against the usual view in which Calvin is the bulwark of a conservative doctrine of Scripture, I argue that he really develops a high view. He is eager to lift the Bible above any human controls, especially in order to free himself from the argument that the church determines the Bible's authority, what it contains, and how to interpret it. At this point we may take one of two paths: the conservative and well-trodden one that passes by the usual guideposts of inerrancy and infallibility, or a much more radical one that really takes seriously the texts condemning oppression, urging collective and inclusive living, and promising justice for the oppressed and retribution for the oppressors. If we grant Calvin's high view of Scripture, then these radical texts must be heeded.

---

1. There are of course plenty of rather traditional theological tensions with which he deals: God and man (Christ's two natures), the Old and New Testaments, free will and determinism, prefall nobility versus postlapsarian depravity, false gods and angels, and so on. However, I am interested in those tensions that emerge at the intersections of Calvin's theological and political thought.

As for grace, the more Calvin emphasizes our depraved and corrupt nature, and the more he stresses that we cannot do a thing for ourselves that might nudge us on the path to salvation, then the more grace becomes a transforming action that revolutionalizes our very being, replacing our hearts of stone with hearts of flesh. Yet just when grace can really do its most radical work of re-creation, Calvin tightens the leash and tells grace what it can and cannot do. On the question of Christian freedom, Calvin sets out to stipulate what such freedom really means: freedom from the law and for Christ; the freedom of inner compulsion that is liberated from external enforcement; and the freedom from any concern with external observances. Here, too, as freedom is about to leap out and become truly radical, Calvin closes the gate: Christian freedom applies only to one's private spiritual life and not to public temporal life.

The fourth great theme is politics, and in this case my concern is the last section of the *Institutes* (4.20.32), where for all his efforts to stipulate obedience to rulers, he closes with the realization that one is duty bound to *disobey* any ungodly and tyrannical ruler. Here I follow Calvin's struggle, moving through his assertions that one must obey at any cost, through recognizing that God and/or his appointed agents may punish and overthrow tyrannical rulers, to his direction not to obey any ungodly ruler. Needless to say, the last absorbs me the most.[2]

My argument moves on to position Calvin in relation to the Bible and particularly to Paul. Calvin was, I argue, too good a student of the Bible not to pick up its multivocality (despite himself, for he tried as hard as he could to read it in a univocal sense). In Paul's case, we find a similar tension between radical and conservative elements, for he too unleashed a radical idea of grace only to take fright at what the various churches did with it. He then sought to rein it back in with a series of qualifications. After pointing out that Calvin has picked up this tension from Paul, my argument moves on to suggest that there is a deeper connection between Paul and Calvin, namely, their analogous situations. Both of them were attempting theological resolutions of profound political and economic contradictions of their respective

---

2. Although the themes I have chosen are major structural pieces of Calvin's theology, they are by no means exhaustive. There are a good number of other topics that I was sorely tempted to pursue, but my sense is that they would have detracted from the main argument. I think of the long discussion of idols (*Inst.* 1:11–12), which initially appears rather quaint and a little archaic in our own day but then on further reflection would offer a distinct perspective on the "society of the spectacle" (Debord 1995), the worship of the image and reification under capitalism. Then there was the connection between special providence and nature that sparks the possibility of a somewhat greenish Calvin and his possible entry into the ecocritical debates (see *Inst.* 1.16 and Dommen 2007).

situations. In each case these tensions turn up in their writings at the level of their theological arguments.

I close the book with a more speculative question: What if we let the radical theological cat out of the bag? By breaking open the tension and letting the Bible, grace, freedom, and Calvin's political thought have their collective head, I offer a picture of what this radical Calvin might look like.

This study is primarily a close reading of the *Institutes*. I am not interested in stringing together endless quotations in the manner of proof texts, nor do I provide a rational paraphrase of Calvin's arguments. There are enough of those efforts around, so I see no need to repeat them. Even more, I do not seek the key to Calvin in his historical, social, intellectual, and theological context. Vitally important that such work is, it also lays down traps for the unwary: if we are not careful, we assume that the secret to understanding Calvin lies in his context. What such approaches miss are the intricacies of Calvin's own text. So my primary approach is actual exegesis and literary analysis with a view to unwinding the complexities of his texts.

So much will I say concerning the argument of the book. Underlying this book is another agenda: to press the point that Calvin's reflections on politics, economics, and society are intimately connected with his theological thought. Although there is a small but steady stream of studies that make precisely this point (Graham 1978; Stevenson 1999), all too often his thought (or indeed anyone's thought) is placed in neat little boxes quite separate from one another (see Höpfl 1982, 217). We have politics here, culture there, economics a little further away, theology around the back, and so on. And often we descend into fruitless arguments about what is the ultimately determining instance. Economics is the key to Calvin's thought, one will cry; no, it is theology, replies another; but no, it is his psychology, argues another. On it goes. In what follows I want to break open those little boxes and let Calvin's various theological and political thoughts fraternize with one another. In fact, I have found that politics and theology interlink very smoothly in Calvin's thought.[3]

---

3. Despite my complaints about the compartmentalizing of studies of Calvin—his theology goes here, his economic thought there and so on—I have profited from some of the studies of his economic, social, and political thought. Especially useful has been Edward Dommen and James B. Bratt's collection *John Calvin Rediscovered: The Impact of His Social and Economic Thought* (Dommen and Bratt 2007). This collection seeks to draw attention to Calvin's thought on social and economic matters and show how that thought has influenced subsequent developments. See also the massive study by Biéler (2006). And then there is Dale K. Van Kley's *The Religious Origins of the French Revolution: From Calvin to the Civil Constitution 1560–1791* (Van Kley 1999). This is a well-documented historical study of the way religious debates beginning with Calvin shaped those in politics, especially in the lead-up to the French Revolution.

Perhaps we can approach this question from the angle of another significant piece from our time of troubles: the conflict between a Christian West and a Muslim East. Broadly speaking, there are two responses to the global tensions we face: either religious language is a cover for other real social, political, and economic issues (a materialist position); or religion is the primary issue and the political, social, and economic issues are secondary (an idealist position). Either the global tensions between Muslim-majority states and nominally Christian or Jewish ones are really political and economic, and the theological language used is a screen, or what we have now is the latest phase of long and deep religious conflict that predates the modern world. If the latter is true, then we are at loggerheads because of fundamentally opposing worldviews (Islam versus Christianity). The connection with Calvin is not difficult to make: either his theological thought is primary and determines all his other reflections on civil society, or his theological language is a cover for basic political and social questions.

It seems to me that both approaches are wrong. Why? They separate the spheres of politics, society, economics, religion, culture, and so on. This is nothing less than a Taylorization of thought, a fragmentation that afflicts us in so many ways. (Taylorization was the process of separating the production process into discrete parts, a method Henry Ford was famous for implementing and perfecting.) So we find people arguing until they are hoarse over whether religion or economic disparity is the main cause of conflict.

Instead, I would suggest that these distinct realms are really not that separate after all. We are far too used to the idea that once upon a time politics, religion, economics, and culture were all mixed up together, but when we grew up as a human society, we separated them all into their neat little categories. Politics is what our politicians do and what specialists analyze; economics is what the merchants and stock markets do; culture is what we find at the art gallery, museum, or cinema. And religion is what the churches and synagogues and mosques and temples and shrines do. My study of Calvin leads me to suggest that we need to drop this harmful approach and realize that such a Taylorization is a fiction. Calvin's theology and politics are in an intimate embrace.

CONTEXT

This argument does not take place on an uninhabited island, unrelated to what goes on around it. There are roughly four groups who form the context for this study. To begin with, there are those who assume the underlying assumption of Max Weber's classic *The Protestant Ethic and the Spirit of Capitalism*: namely, that in some sense Calvin is one of the fathers of modern, capitalist society with its liberal ideology.[4] As is well known, Weber argued that the Protestant Reformation paved the way for capitalism by means of a thorough change of beliefs and daily habits of life. Weber was particularly interested in Calvin and Calvinism, for there he found the process through which monastic disciplines—the ordered day of work, frugal living, asceticism, self-denial, the calling to a religious life, individualism, predestination, the dependence on God's grace by human beings who were utterly incapable of any good themselves yet were constantly impelled to good works in response to that grace—made their way out of the monasteries and into the population at large. These patterns of daily life were crucial in making the large shift from medieval patterns to those more suited to capitalism. While Luther took the first step in the breakdown of medieval monasticism, Calvin's contribution was to make this world a place of testing and preparation for life in another world that cannot be known as yet. One's daily life then became the scene for an unprecedented rationalization, whereby every moment was subject to ordering, scrutiny, and accountability. The paradox here is that Calvin did not make human life less religious; rather, the whole of human life became a monastery. Yet it was exactly this comprehensive religionization that produced both the possibilities for capitalism and the demise of Calvinist Protestantism as such. For by sacralizing the whole of life, Calvinism also rationalizes it (a rationalizing inherent in the monasteries abolished by Luther). Having enabled such a worldly asceticism, there is no longer any need for the religious content to remain. A purely secular ascetism becomes the logical outcome of Calvin's theology, which can then be discarded once it has done its job. Calvinist Protestantism thereby functions as a catalytic agent that disappears once its task is over. Calvinism is, in other words, a "vanishing mediator."

All this may well be true. Indeed, at an anecdotal level (which really boils down to watching my parents and their friends) it seems to me that Weber was correct to some extent. But it also seems that he missed a crucial feature of Calvin: that he struggled with the tension between the radical implications of his theology and the desire to contain those

---

4. These studies keep rolling off the presses. See the excellent essay by Sara Farris, "The 'Individual' of Social Change: The Anti-Authoritarian Nature of Modernity in Max Weber" (2007). The list is almost endless, but let me note Bryan Turner (1999), Stephen Turner (2000), Bendix (1998), Hamilton (1991), Yinger (1980), Parkin (2003), Sayer (1990), Hancock (1989), du Cros (1999), Graham (1978, 189–201), McGrath (1990, 219–46), Stückelberger (2007), and Tawney (1926).

implications. In other words, there is a radical edge to Calvin that does not fit the picture Weber paints of him and his influence.[5]

A second context and inspiration for this study is the loose group of contemporary philosophers who have revived the idea of political theology. While they all promote their own agendas, they do share one assumption: the texts of the Bible, especially the Letters of Paul, are vitally important political texts—not merely in Paul's own time (the concern of too many biblical critics), but now, in our own time. None of these characters are biblical scholars by any stretch of the imagination. But what they bring to Paul's texts are philosophical and political concerns that bring Paul to life and make him vitally important.

This broadening debate began with a Frenchman, a Slovenian, an Italian, and a German. The first was Alain Badiou, who began the recent spate of interest in political theology with his effort to recover a laicized and militant grace in Paul's letters (Badiou 2003, 1997). Not long afterwards Slavoj Žižek responded with a series of encounters that ranged, somewhat haphazardly, over Christian love, ethics, and grace (Žižek 1999, 2001, 2003; Žižek, Santner, and Reinhard 2006; Žižek and Milbank 2009). And in Italy, Giorgio Agamben responded with his own study that focused on the messianic and remnant elements of Paul's thought (Agamben 2000, 2005).[6] In each case, there is an urgency driven by the strong sense that, for political reasons, Paul is more relevant than ever in our own day and age. The same sense pervades the study by Jacob Taubes (2004), originally a series of lectures given in 1987 as he was dying from cancer. Taubes argued for an apocalyptic-revolutionary reading of Paul. From there the debate has blossomed, generating a spate of secondary commentary of which *Paul in Philosophy and Culture* (Blanton and De Vries, forthcoming) is probably the best. There is the inevitable search for lesser-known but no less important voices, such as Bernard Sichère (2003) and Shmuel Trigano (2003). And then we have the recovery of a philosophical tradition of reflections on Paul, a tradition that has worked largely outside biblical studies and theology and has preferred to refer to its own predecessors. Heidegger, for one, reflected at length on Paul (2004, 47–111), and Kristeva kept returning to a Paul she clearly likes for his invention of the new collective, the *ekklēsia*, and his ability to deal with a host of psychological pathologies through the story of the

---

5. As Michael Löwy points out (1992, 14–15), Weber (1952) identified an antiauthoritarian streak in Judaism, especially with the challenge to patriarchal authority in the name of a higher one. But Weber did not make the same point for Calvinism.

6. See the detailed discussions in my *Criticism of Heaven* (Boer 2007b) and *Criticism of Religion* (Boer, in press).

death and resurrection of Jesus (Kristeva 1983, 135–47; 1987, 139–50; 1988, 113–22; 1991, 83). I could go on, but I think I have said enough to show that this is a lively debate and one that is not about to subside any time soon. It seems that the political theology—or as I prefer to call it, the revolutionary theology—of Calvin should be heard in this debate, too. He is too important to be ignored.

A third context for my argument is made up of scholars and specialists in Calvin. There is always the risk that I will be dismissed as not being a scholar of Calvin—whatever that means. I dabble in biblical scholarship and political philosophy, but have not made my home in Calvin or Reformation scholarship or any of the other subspecialties that we like to create in our endless division of labor into ever-smaller fields. In fact, I suspect that Calvin would have looked with horror at the Taylorized academic marketplace that we inhabit in this period of late capitalism. He would have found our knowledge factories abhorrent, where scholars are assigned their little posts, tightening bolts or polishing the exterior of yet another product for intellectual consumption. Or to shift the metaphor, we burrow down into ever-smaller areas, occasionally blinking at the light when we look up or out. And we each guard our little hole ever more jealously, whether it be biblical criticism, systematic theology, history, homiletics, or some other subspecialty.

The problem is that Calvin himself cannot be contained in such a way. To whom does he belong? Is he the preserve of church historians with a specialty in the Reformation? Or does he belong to systematic theologians with their own interest in Calvin? Is he the sole property of Reformed churches who claim his heritage? Is he the preserve of homiletic specialists because of his endless sermons? Or is he only for those who claim a Reformed background, in terms of either religious commitment or the way they were brought up? Can biblical scholars claim him because of his extensive commentaries on the Bible and because they can assess with some skill his exegetical ability? Or is he the domain of philosophers who are all too aware of Calvin's philosophical credentials?

I can actually claim some modest experience and skills as well as a number of publications in the last two or three categories, for biblical criticism is my bread and butter, and political philosophy, my abiding passion. I was brought up in a Reformed context, living and breathing Calvin for much of my life, and I have dabbled in theology, so perhaps that could be added to the list. In fact, I would suggest that those of us who are restless when contained within one small subdiscipline, who are always roaming through the plains and mountains of other fields, might actually have more in common with Calvin than at first seems to be the case.

The last context for this study is actually a subgroup of the previous one. It is a somewhat motley collection of Calvin scholars who are by far the most interesting—those who argue that Calvin is "revolutionary."[7] Precisely what "revolution" means is not quite clear, especially when every week brings some revolutionary design for toothbrushes or toilet cleaners or what have you. Here we need to invoke the old distinction between revolution and reform. While revolution is the sweeping away of the old and beginning anew, reform is that tinkering with the system to make it work better—although one must always ask, by whom and for whom? Like those toothbrushes, we sometimes find the word "revolution" used for what is actually reform. This is where I place those studies that see Calvin as a progressive (Biéler 1964; 2006), as a forefather of secularized modernity by providing a viable link between reason and revelation (Hancock 1989), or of liberal democracy (McNeill 1949; du Cros 1999; Kelly 1992), or of human rights and modern practices of education (du Cros 1999), or even the structure of governance (Kingdon 1975). To be sure, there are elements of Calvin's thought that lead in these directions, but such arguments tend to be apologetic ("Calvin isn't the stern authoritarian you thought he was, and these developments are all good for us"), or provide another somewhat gentler angle on Weber's argument that Calvin is important for the developing ideology and practice of capitalism.

Of those who understand revolution for what it is—a drastically destructive and constructive process that rearranges the coordinates by which we live—we find differing positions that may be roughly distinguished as follows: (1) Calvin is a key player in the bourgeois revolution that ushered in capitalism; (2) he is one of those dreadful fanatical revolutionaries; or (3) his revolutionary possibilities run up against his conservatism. The "bourgeois revolution" option is really a radicalizing of Weber's argument. In this case, the "vanishing mediator" becomes the agent of thorough social and economic transformation. For example, R. H. Tawney (1926, 102–32) argues that Calvin rearranged the very coordinates of life by making works the necessary element of sanctification and a sign of God's grace, by stressing individualism, by becoming

---

7. Over against the idea of a revolutionary Calvin, some argue that Calvin was a judgmental authoritarian and unbending traditionalist (Allen 1941; Hancock 1989) or at least that he wasn't all that progressive (Höpfl 1982, 193–94).

the ideology of mobile merchants, and by overturning many medieval assumptions concerning social institutions and practice. This position is both well known and limited: Is Calvin an agent or symptom of such change? And what do we do with his deep conservatism?

Tawney ends up being unimpressed with Calvin, but that is nothing compared with those who see his brand of revolution as the scourge of the modern world. For Michael Walzer (1965), Calvin is one of the most important in a long list of dangerous and deluded zealots, especially those Puritans who ended up overthrowing the monarchy in England through a judicial murder. Needless to say, the misguided Walzer is not one for revolutions, and the term carries a distinct odium. The same applies to Eric Voegelin (1952, 131–40), for whom Calvin was a gnostic revolutionary whose thought and practice leads straight to totalitarianism. In other words, for this type of argument "revolution" designates the dangerous destructiveness of rabid radicals. One of the problems (there are many) with this position is that one part of Calvin would agree; he would point out the trait in others and let fly with invective.

Finally, there are a few scholars who identify some structural tensions in Calvin's thought, tensions between external enforcement and the inner life (Little 1986), between determinism and agency (Graham 1978, 185), between a traditionalist anxious about change and an opportunist who was a revolutionary in spite of himself (Bousma 1988), or between progressive democrat and traditional authoritarian (Stevenson 1999). Let me say some more about each, since I have mined them deeply. With Little (1986), I agree that there is an unresolved tension between the temporal and the spiritual realms (Calvin's terms), or between establishmentarianism and the inner life (Little's terms). Sometimes Calvin argues that the state should enforce religious practice, and at other times he asserts that the spiritual life is above any interference from the state. However, I do not agree that the unstable nature of this tension is the secret to the destabilizing and renovating effect of Calvin's legacy. Rather, what Little has drawn out is one form of the deep struggle within Calvin's thought, a struggle that would continue to show up in Calvinism's ongoing contradictions. This means that I agree even less with Stevenson (1999), for whom such tensions are a normal part of living the Christian faith and a source of its creativity. I appreciate the way Stevenson brings out the progressive-traditional dichotomy, pushing it at times to the sharper tension of revolutionary and reactionary. But to see it all woven together in a neat, creative, and pious package is going too far.

I am drawn more to Bousma's (1988) psychological portrait of Calvin, especially because of the way he stresses the unresolved clash between the inflexible conservative and the flexible opportunist and the way he links these warring tendencies of the "two Calvins" to both his context and psychological makeup. The problem is that Bousma is too enamored with his psychological search and is content to rest his argument on the shaky basis of an anxious Calvin. On top of that I find the use of Calvin's texts as a source of historical information wanting: it is a flat reading of texts that seems more like rationalist paraphrase than close attention to the texts' literary intricacies. I am closest to Graham (1978, 185), who sees an unresolved tension between determinism and revolutionary agency (predestination and responsibility), a tension he also sees in the mix of voluntarism and inevitability of Marx. Unfortunately, this is only a minor point with Graham's robust book, which breathes the excitement and urgency of the 1960s. It opens with a bold statement that Calvin was the "leader of a revolution" (1978, 11) at all levels of society, then dares to make a few cautious connections with Marx (209), but finally whittles away Calvin's revolutionary credentials with one qualification after another. Graham really wants to recover a liberal, social-justice Calvin who adds a moral element to our secularized, commercial lives. Although I am sympathetic to the way Graham sees Calvin as a (somewhat moderate) revolutionary—and in this respect he follows a long tradition that includes Georges Sorel (1961, 124–25) and Antonio Gramsci (1996, 142, 243–44)—it seems to me that the tensions within Calvin's thought and practice are crucial to understanding his radicalism.

Thus these four underlying currents or, if you like, overlapping fields—Weber enthusiasts, a revived political theology, and Calvin scholars with a bent for locating tensions in his thought—will meet in this study for a bit of conversation, argument, and perhaps a few steps forward.

SENTENCE PRODUCTION

Most of what follows is concerned with the scholar's bread and butter, namely, content. Yet I have always been seduced by questions of style or, as I prefer, sentence production. How do writers construct phrases, sentences, and whole passages? Are the sentences short, punchy ones or long, looping efforts? Is the style plodding and flat-footed, or does it take off and draw you in? Do writers feel constrained by thoughts of reception and the genre in which they write, or do they let loose with a devil-may-care attitude? Do they write quickly in order to let the subconscious have a say, or do they labor over each sentence, lovingly bringing it to perfection? For Calvin, the answer must be that it was a little bit of each. He tried to write in a careful and ordered fashion, but the problem was that he wrote far too quickly (he did after all write himself to death), and in the rush he was unable to keep a lid on everything.

When we look closely at Calvin's sentences, a curious pattern emerges. There is the patient and pedantic Calvin, one who constructs his sentences, paragraphs, and chapters in a predictable and rather simple form. He briefly states his main point, sometimes including a summary of his preceding argument, and then provides a fuller explanation and often a good dose of polemic against opponents. He then selects biblical passages that back up his argument and more often than not seeks to untangle some paradox or other, usually in conversation with one or more figures—Augustine, say, or John Chrysostom or Pelagius. And he has a great love for the methodical exposition of items such as the Ten Commandments and the Lord's Prayer (*Inst.* 2.8; *OS* 3:343–98; *Inst.* 3.20.34–48; *OS* 4:344–65). Soon enough you know what to expect. Not a bad pedagogical device, although it is somewhat plodding and does get tedious.[8]

One of the most telling strategies in this ordered sentence production is his strategy of identifying two extremes and then walking a line between them. As he puts it elsewhere, "The best way to avoid error will be to consider the perils that threaten on both sides" (*Inst.* 2.2.1; *OS* 3:241.10–12; translation modified). It may be anarchy or tyranny, works and grace, freedom and legalism, Anabaptism or Rome, quietism or libertinage as a result of justification by faith, or any of the endless parade of extremes he cites. Often one gains the impression that he is beset on either side by thickets of error. It is a brilliant rhetorical strategy, for it makes him seem reasonable and moderate. Here are two extremes, he says, but I will seek the moderate path between them. I must admit to having used this strategy on a number of occasions, especially when I have wanted to present a radical position. Simply claim the center ground by identifying what was the center as an extreme, and before long the audience is on your side.

Apart from the careful ordering of his text, there is another type of sentence production going on in Calvin's works. Every now and then

---

8. This is the Calvin whom all too many commentators follow. In the same way Calvin refers endlessly to the Bible, so also they refer endlessly to Calvin.

the reader's eyes light on an extraordinary image or metaphor, a vivid description or a piece of delightfully vicious polemic. These moments burst out of the careful sentences and take one by surprise. Suddenly we come across some flair, some burning passion that Calvin usually keeps on a tight rein. But every now and then it shakes its head as if to break free. Let me give a few examples.

To begin with, this wonderful passage might well be subtitled "The Pursuit of Unhappiness":

> Consequently, unhappy consciences find no rest from being troubled and tossed by a terrible whirlwind, from feeling that they are being torn asunder by a hostile Deity, pierced and lanced by deadly darts, quaking at God's lightning bolt, and being crushed by the weight of his hand—so that it would be more bearable to go down into any bottomless depths and chasms than to stand for a moment in these terrors. What and how great is this, to be eternally and unceasingly besieged by him?
>
> (*Inst.* 3.25.12; *OS* 4:456.18–24)

What a wonderful read! As is the following description of the calamities that may befall us:

> Various diseases repeatedly trouble us: now plague rages; now we are cruelly beset by the calamities of war; now ice and hail, consuming the year's expectation, lead to barrenness, which reduces us to poverty; wife, parents, children, neighbors, are snatched away by death; our house is burned by fire. It is on account of these occurrences that men curse their life, loathe the day of their birth, abominate heaven and the light of day, rail against God, and as they are eloquent in blasphemy, accuse him of injustice and cruelty. But in these matters the believer must also look to God's kindness and truly fatherly indulgence.
>
> (*Inst.* 3.7.10; *OS* 4:160.20–31)

I find myself wondering whether Calvin ever thought about selling insurance policies. And then there are those glorious attacks on enemies and false interpreters. For example, there is the attack on the use of images of the saints and virgins by the Roman Catholics: "Brothels show harlots clad more virtuously and modestly than the churches show those objects which they wish to be thought images of virgins" (*Inst.* 1.11.7; *OS* 3:93.11–12). And his colorful description of monasteries: "This is clear: that no order of men is more polluted by all sorts of foul vices; nowhere do factions, hatreds, party zeal, and intrigue burn more fiercely" (*Inst.* 4.13.15; *OS* 5:252.24–27). Or we find the petulant who "belch forth [*evomere*] blasphemies by which to obscure heaven" (*Inst.* 1.14.1; *OS* 3:153.18–19) and the "foul grunting of the swine" who blaspheme against predestination (*Inst.* 3.23.12; *OS* 4:406.21). He reserves his greatest invective for the Church of Rome, calling its priests adulterers, whoremongers, and even "bastards" (*Inst.* 4.5.6; *OS* 5:79.30); calling its bishops rude and ignorant (*Inst.* 4.12.21; *OS* 5:230.13–14), and the pope himself the Antichrist. Myriad are these moments in Calvin's texts, and it makes them a sheer pleasure to read. The man could certainly write, and I often ponder using such turns of phrase ("furious madmen" and "petulant scoffers" are my favorites) to denounce an opponent or someone with whom I disagree.

Inevitably, sentence style touches on content, for the two cannot be completely separated. Calvin's style, or what I like to call sentence production, is an extraordinarily revealing instance of the argument of this book: under normal circumstances, he liked to keep things under control, to maintain careful order. I can imagine that Calvin's day would be structured in a calm and careful fashion, that he would hang his washing in groups (underwear, robes, caps, socks) and in ascending order of size. But then something would break out, some concealed passion or flare of anger or deep pleasure. Here it is a literary flourish, an image or metaphor that sparks the imagination, or polemical outburst that disrupts the calm surface of the text, or even the structure of a sentence itself. Indeed, at times we actually find this very pattern embodied in a sentence or two: "I only say that through the stupid hardness of their hearts, which the impious eagerly conjure up to reject God, wastes away, yet the sense of divinity, which they greatly wished to have extinguished, is still in vigour, *and now and then it breaks forth*" (*Inst.* 1.3.3; *OS* 3:40.7–10; translation and emphasis mine). Ostensibly, Calvin writes of the wicked who yet cannot resist the breaking out of a sense of God. But the *form* of the sentence is exactly what I have found happens in Calvin's theological arguments: despite his best efforts, a vigorous radical sense now and then breaks forth. So it is also with the tension between the revolutionary and conservative elements of his political theology: the former breaks forth every now and then despite the best efforts of the latter.

1
Protesting Too Much

My concern, then, is the tension between the radical possibilities of Calvin's thought and his efforts to contain those possibilities. In order to uncover this tension, layer by layer, I resort to a strategy of picking up some key texts. They may be made up of a sentence or two, or they may be slightly longer, but they capture one after another what I seek. I have chosen the texts carefully, for they provide windows into the deep struggle within Calvin's thought. While I exegete these texts closely, I also provide references to other points in Calvin's work where similar ideas turn up. Imagine, if you will, a solitary skateboarder at a skate park (like the ones I see at the park by the beach near me). Soon, others turn up, wanting to join in. Ones and twos continue to arrive, joining in the leaping, skidding, hopping, and aerial acrobatics until the skate park is full. I follow a similar pattern in my analysis of Calvin's texts.

I begin with a brief statement of my argument in this chapter: In the context of the political and religious upheavals of Europe, Calvin pleads that what he preaches is not rebellion. However, by trying to counter the assertions of his opponents that he seeks to "turn everything upside down" (LCC 1:10; *OS* 3:10.16), it seems to me that he protests too much. Here is the key text that I wish to subject to close analysis. It comes from the letter that opens the *Institutes*, addressed to Francis I, king of France:

> So that no one may think we are wrongly complaining of these things, you can be our witness, most noble King, how with many

lying slanders it is daily traduced in your presence. It is as if this doctrine looked to no other end than to wrest the scepters from the hands of kings, to cast down all courts and judgments, to subvert all orders and civil governments, to disrupt the peace and quiet of the people, to abolish all laws, to scatter all lordships and possessions—in short, to turn everything upside down!

(LCC 1:10; emphasis added)

Nequis haec iniuria nos queri existimet, ipse nobis testis esse potes, Rex nobilissime, quam mendacibus calumniis quotodie apud te traducatur, quod non aliorsum spectet nisi ut Regibus sua sceptra e manibus extorqueat, tribunalia, iudiciaque omnia praecipitet, subvertat ordines omnes et politias, pacem et quietem populi perturbet, leges omnes abroget, dominia et possessiones dissipet, omnia denique sursum deorsum volvat.

(*OS* 3:10.10–16)

Now let us delve into and consider this passage in more detail. The biblical critic in me wishes to look at the text first; the historian wants context; and the theologian within seeks a contradiction or two. Rather than listening to many voices at once, however, I will give each a fair go.

EXEGESIS

Exegesis first: this text has three steps. It begins with the claim that it is perfectly fair to defend oneself, moves on to state that what has been said against the author is a pure lie, and then outlines the content of that lie. Rather than following the run of a text and allowing it to dominate, I prefer to resist that flow and begin in reverse. The reason for doing so is that the ability of a text (and indeed an author) to persuade is closely connected to the way a text flows. And Calvin is a master rhetorician and thereby a master of persuasion.

So I begin at the end, with the content of the "cunning lies" (*mendacibus calumniis*). The verbs are muscular: Calvin and his cohorts want to "wrest" (*extorqueat*), "cast down" (*praecipitet*), "subvert" (*subvertat*), "disrupt" (*perturbet*), "abolish" (*abroget*), and "scatter" (*dissipet*). Often when I read Calvin I have the sense that the man didn't know quite when to stop writing, or indeed how to say anything succinctly. However, this flow of verbs has a distinct rhetorical effect, and I for one am pleased he let his quill run on. One gains the impression of the cut of a sword or perhaps the systematic acts of destruction of a rebel army. They are thorough. One by one the institutions of the old, corrupt order are done away with. Cast down, subvert, abolish—they are not merely the terms of wanton destruction or criminal vandalism (the accusations reactionaries constantly make against revolutionaries). Rather, they are the terminology of insurrection and revolution. Above all, we have the last phrase that sums up the list: to "turn everything upside down" (*omnia . . . sursum deorsum volvat*).

I would like to spend a moment with these various Latin verbs, since Calvin's choice of them is not mere literary flourish. The underlying sense of *extorqueo* is to use force in order to acquire something from someone else. We can imagine someone wrenching, tearing, or twisting something out of another's hands. As for *praecipito* (usually translated as "cast down" or "overturn"), the sense is one of violently hurling or throwing something down. It can end up meaning to hurry and rush (hence "precipitate"), but in this case I have a picture of something hurled down in anger and broken in pieces, much like Moses and the tablets of the law on Mt Sinai. Then we have *subverto*. All too easily it gives us the English "subvert," but it helps matters if I mention that it includes the senses of overturning and overthrowing. In other words, it is a very good revolutionary term. As for *perturbo*, the usual translation as "disrupt" or "disturb" is a little gentle—you may disturb my reading, I may have a disrupted sleep, or you may be bothered by something. *Perturbo* can be stronger than that, with the sense of throwing into disorder and confounding. *Abrogo* is next: it means to annul or repeal, and it relates directly to laws. *Dissipo* is another powerful verb, with the sense of scattering, routing, and putting to flight. The immediate picture it conjures up is of a beaten and shattered army, in full flight from the enemy.

Tearing, hurling down, overthrowing, confounding, repealing, and routing—to be completely blunt, these verbs speak of revolution. Calvin himself gives us as good a definition as you will find of revolution: "turn all things upside down" (*omnia . . . sursum deorsum volvat*), or more literally, to make everything, up and down, revolve. Or in a slightly more extended version, to shake up everything so that the lowly are lifted up and the haughty are cast down. The echo of the Magnificat of Luke 1 is no accident—"He has put down the mighty from their thrones, and exalted those of low degree"(v. 52 RSV)—for that is precisely the image Calvin conjures up. Add to this the fact that the Latin verb *volvo* is actually at the heart of the word revolution, and Calvin has hit the nail pretty much on the head.

So with Calvin's assistance we can now define *revolution* as the thorough shaking up and overthrow of a complete political, social, and economic system and its replacement with another. I will have more to say on this definition later, but it will already be clear that it is not merely a palace coup—one section of the ruling class (a few disgruntled nobles) lops off the heads of another section, seizes power, and everything continues as before. A little like what passes for parliamentary democracy. . . .

However, I have run ahead of myself. There is another dimension to these phrases, namely, the objects of the verbs. What is torn out, thrown down, overthrown, confounded, annulled, and routed? These are the scepters of kings, courts and judgments, order and government, the peace of society and laws, and lordships and possessions. As before, I take each one in turn.

Calvin's list begins with the scepters of kings. As symbols of power that one wants to twist and tear out of the hands of kings, the comment is obvious (and would have existential relevance for Francis I). Next, we find that courts and judgments, or seats of justice, are being hurled to the ground and dashed in pieces. Before we rush in to picture our secular judicial system, carefully demarcated from the church courts that still carry on a ghostly presence and pretend they have jurisdiction, I would point out that when Calvin refers to courts and seats of justice, he means a very different judicial system. Here it is a judiciary administered by the nobles for the nobles. Peasants might try to gain some justice, but it was usually a forlorn effort. And the church courts still had the power of life and death, especially in terms of heresy. Closely connected is the annulment of all laws. Once again, in order to get a sense of what this means, we need a paradigm shift: not only is the body of canon law at issue, but the idea that the laws of the land derive in some way from the Bible and divine law also is still very strong.

So far we have kings shorn of power, the judiciary smashed, and laws null and void. At this point anarchy and chaos show their ugly faces—at least for the purveyors of order and control. This sense of chaos continues with the effort to put to flight and scatter the lordships (*dominia*) and possessions (*possessiones*), or as I prefer, distinctions of rank or status and property. The assumption here is that the social and economic ordering of society is determined by the amount of landed property one possesses. You still hear the comment every now and then that the best thing to do with your money (if you happen to have any) is to buy real estate. The sense of solidity and permanence is still conveyed by the English term *real* estate. However, in these days of financialization and speculation, the desire for such landed property is really nostalgia for a bygone era. And that era is the one Calvin inhabits, where one's position in the social hierarchy was carefully controlled, legislated, and as far as possible, fixed.

The final two items are the peace and quiet of the people (*pacem et quietem populi*) and the pair of orders and governments (*ordines omnes et politias*). The former sounds all too familiar, for how often do we hear complaints that someone or other is disrupting the peace and quiet—teenagers out drinking on a Friday night, hoods tearing up and down the road in their cars, unwashed hippies protesting against something or other, women calling for a minimal equality, indigenous peoples crying for justice.... The catch is that such peace and quiet is all too often a thin veneer that covers a system of corruption and violent repression.

I have left the *ordines* and *politias* until last. Usually translated as "orders" and "governments," the senses of these words are richer than that. While *ordo* originally means a row or line, it has a distinctly military sense of rank as well as a social one of class. As for *politia*, it is a direct copy from the Greek *politeia*, whose root is *polis*. Rather than merely the government, it really designates all matters of the body politic—citizens, executives, and various forms of government. *Politia* thus concerns the way of ordering the political life of any society. This is where the additional "*omnes*" is crucial: *omnes ordines*, writes Calvin. *All* the ways of structuring and ordering the political life of society are under threat and about to be overturned. In Calvin's own words, they are the ones that are not merely replacing one type of government with another, but also altering the coordinates, revolutionizing the basic reference points of politics. It is, in other words, a thoroughgoing revolution.

I have traced these various items through in some detail not merely because I like exegeting texts, but also because they each refer to one piece of a total social and economic system. But what is that system? The obvious answer is that it comprises a king, judiciary, people, laws, an ordered body politic, and a carefully organized and guarded ranking of people in terms of landed property. In a little more detail, the pieces of this social and economic structure are (1) the monarch, who is the leading figure among the nobility but not yet an absolute monarch;[1] (2) the judicial system in which nobles and the church administered "justice" according

---

1. The push to an absolute monarchy and state over against the power of the nobles and the first pockets of the bourgeoisie happened after the Renaissance, although the seeds were certainly there earlier (see Anderson 1979). Indeed, while Lutheran thought, especially in the hands of Melanchthon and the doctrine of the two kingdoms, gave a strong impetus to absolute monarchies such as that of Denmark and Prussia, Calvin's thought implied a limitation to the monarch that would undermine absolute monarchy. See further my discussion in chapter 5.

to laws that favored or penalized one according to one's position in the social hierarchy and whose purpose was to ensure and protect that hierarchy; (3) a ranking in society that worked its way up from the serfs at the base along with landless free laborers, journeymen and artisans at the next level, the clergy, and then the nobility, of whom the monarch was merely the most powerful; and (4) a body politic that relied on an unequal mutual give-and-take between lord and serf (produce and land rent for one, land to cultivate and protection for another), between parish priest and bishop, and between nobles and the king. To keep such a hierarchy from too much disturbance, to ensure that everyone by and large remained in his or her station in life—this was the *pax et quietes populi* of which Calvin speaks. In its totality this is what usually goes by the name of a feudal social formation. What Calvin has done with his rhetorical list of threatened items is provide a neat picture of medieval feudal society.

CONTEXT

I did promise that there would be more than some detailed exegesis of the preface addressed to Francis I of France. At the beginning of this chapter I set out to satisfy the biblical exegete, the historian, and the theologian within me. The biblical critic may be happy for now, but the others remain to be satisfied. As far as the historian is concerned, I have already slipped into context in the closing comments of my exegesis. However, that brief picture of feudal society is more synchronic than diachronic; in that sense it is an ideal type distilled from the messy experiences of everyday life. The strange breed known as historians will want some more specificity, especially of a diachronic kind.[2] There are three important items here: Calvin alludes to the *Affaire des Placards* of 1534, the Peasants' War of 1525, and the Münster Revolution that was taking place at the same time that he was writing this prefatory epistle to Francis I of France. Let me say a little more about each one.

Affaire des Placards

The Placards Affair was actually the immediate reason Calvin had to leave France. During the crackdown in the aftermath of the affair, when

---

2. Among others of that strange breed, see Mentzer and Spicer (2002), Benedict (2002), and Skinner (1978).

the Catholic majority was outraged, Francis I affirmed the Roman Catholic faith, Protestants were hunted down, and Calvin and other Protestant leaders were forced to flee. But what was the Placards Affair?

During the night before Sunday, October 18, 1534, anti-Catholic posters appeared in public places in Paris and in the four provincial cities of Blois, Rouen, Tours, and Orléans. Frenchmen arose on Sunday morning to read posters that carried the following title: "Genuine articles on the horrific, great and insupportable [*importable*] abuses of the papal mass, invented directly contrary to the Holy Supper of our Lord, sole mediator and sole savior Jesus Christ."[3] The key words here are "mass" versus "Holy Supper," terms that still mark out one's theological and indeed cultural position. I remember all too clearly the ban on the use of words such as "communion" or "Eucharist," let alone the dreaded "mass," in my parents' household. It was "the Lord's Supper," and that was that.

In France of 1534 these placards were a direct attack on the Roman Catholic doctrine of transubstantiation. They took a Zwinglian line, arguing that the sacrament of the Last Supper was a symbol and nothing more. The author and source of the posters remains unclear, but they seem to have come from Neuchâtel in Switzerland, which would make sense, given their Zwinglian flavor.[4]

Francis I also had a more personal reason to be troubled over the placards. Someone managed to place one on his own bedchamber door at Amboise. The king was, to say the least, not impressed and rather shaken by the thought of someone sneaking past the guards and plastering a poster on his bedroom door as he snored away. The affair brought an end to the relatively liberal policies of Francis, Queen Claude, and the king's sister, Marguerite de Navarre. Part humanist and part reforming, in the early years of the sixteenth century the policy of mild enlightenment had encouraged new ideas and free thinking. Francis had also attempted to protect the Protestants from the harsher measures of the *Parlement de Paris* and the opposition to the reforming push.

With the placards all that came to an end. Roman Catholic processions were organized in all the parishes of Paris for the following Sunday. The king offered a reward for any information that would lead to the arrest of the perpetrator or perpetrators, who were to be

---

3. The French reads, "*Articles véritables sur les horribles, grands et importables* [sic, i.e., insupportables] *abuz de la messe papale, inventée directement contre la Sainte Cène de notre Seigneur, seul médiateur et seul Sauveur Jésus-Christ*" (Berthoud 1973, 287).

4. Some would suggest it was Antoine de Marcourt, a pastor of Neuchâtel; see Berthoud (1973).

burned at the stake. We can easily imagine what followed: without the king's protection, the Protestant minority was no longer safe; the Roman Catholic members of the court and the clergy made the most of the situation; informers came forward; neighborhood squabbles were settled (the owner of that annoying dog across the lane, the old sourpuss around the corner, the man who has been eyeing my wife . . .). Soon enough, the vigilant authorities had locked up a good number of Protestant sympathizers. The trials were brief; justice (as is usual) served the interests of the powerful; convictions were pronounced by November 10; and the first culprit, an unfortunate cripple named Barthélemi Milon, was burned at the stake.

So, in light of this whole business, Calvin wishes to reassure the jumpy Francis I that he and his friends are not of this ilk. *We* won't be going about disrupting the peace of the realm, smashing up law and order, overthrowing the divinely appointed government, dispensing with the medieval privilege of landed property, or—God forbid—grabbing Francis's scepter and deposing him from the throne. Not like those radicals a few cantons over from here—those dreadful Zwinglians! And not like those Anabaptist scoundrels and miscreants. They may plaster threatening posters on your bedroom door. They may threaten revolution and death to the pope and all Roman clergy. But not us!

It seems all too much like the squabbles between different religious groups, or indeed between political cells: one's sworn enemies are invariably those closest to you. You may share 99 percent of the beliefs and practices, but it is the 1 percent that makes you the bitterest of foes. Here in Australia, the bitterness still runs deep between those Presbyterians who decided to join with the Methodists and Congregationalists to form the Uniting Church in 1977 and those who refused and formed the continuing Presbyterian Church. Apart from a few minor points of doctrine and practice, there is little that separates the two. Yet as a child and then teenager during the debates and struggles and votes, I gained the distinct impression from those around me that the gulf separating the "Uniters" and the "Continuers" was so deep and so wide that they may as well have come from different planets. They were certainly going to different places in the afterlife.

As I walk through my university, I see various posters: "Denounce the imperialist war" cries one from the International Socialists; "March against the U.S. occupation of Iraq" shouts another from the Socialist Alternative; "Walk against global scorching" proclaims a poster from the

Green Left.[5] I can't help wondering why these small groups on the Left don't link arms and develop a common front instead of vying with one another for converts. In fact, they often fight for poster space with Christians on Campus, the Catholic Student Society, and Campus Crusade.

Münster Revolution

The Placards Affair had an extra punch to it since it took place during what has become known as the Münster Rebellion or the Kingdom of Münster. Names are important, for they often carry their own judgments, something that has certainly not been lacking with Münster. For that reason I would rather call it the Münster Revolution. For seventeen months, from February 1534 until June 1535, Münster was under the control of radical Anabaptists. During this brief and tumultuous period a communism of goods was instituted (based on Acts 2:44–45; 4:32–35); all non-Anabaptists were expelled or executed; twelve judges were appointed as in Israel of old; the kingdom of David was proclaimed; the self-appointed king, Jan van Leyden, took many wives; Münster was declared the "New Jerusalem"; everyone believed that Christ was about to return to earth with a massive army to wipe out all their enemies; and there were more dreams, visions, and direct encounters with God than the hippies next door can produce in a collective lifetime. Not content with taking over the government of Münster, these radicals set about organizing campaigns to conquer the rest of the world—with God's help of course.

How did all this come about? Münster in 1534 was the confluence of various streams. One that fed into the apocalyptic stream of the Münster rebels was economic hardship and politicotheological persecution. Many of those attracted to Anabaptism came from the poorest levels of the crumbling medieval economies. As is usually the case with transitions between economic systems (in this case from feudalism to the first glimmers of capitalism), economic hardship and social unrest are rife. Add to this the Roman Catholic propensity to pounce upon and eradicate with violence any stirrings of Lutheran thought, and you have

---

5. Those who have seen Monty Python's film *The Life of Brian* will perhaps recall the opening scene, where a small group of three or four men at a Roman circus cast aspersions on the Judean People's Front and the Popular Front of Judea. Their own revolutionary group is the People's Front of Judea. See http://www.youtube.com/watch?v=gb_qHP7VaZE (accessed April 16, 2008).

an increasingly desperate population. It is a classic breeding ground for apocalyptic fervor, desperate measures, and hopes for the return of Christ in light of "the signs of the times." We should also not forget that daily life for many was painful (there was no aspirin or any other effective painkiller), diets were poor, food was unhygienic and potentially hallucinogenic, disease was rife, and death a terrifying experience. For example, it was assumed that Lazarus was thoroughly miserable after Jesus raised him from the dead because he dreaded the thought of dying a second time (Huizinga 1924, 132). In light of these conditions, it should come as no surprise that when Münster was declared the New Jerusalem, many Dutch Anabaptists (Münster is close to the Dutch border) set out in the hope of joining their comrades in the city. Even though many were blocked, arrested, sent back, and executed, a good number of them made it through.

A second stream that fed into the Münster Revolution was the Peasants' Revolt of a decade earlier (1524–1525), about which I will have more to say in a moment. One outcome of the defeat of the Peasant armies and the brutal repression that followed was that the hopes for a lighter burden by the peasants remained unfulfilled. In and around Münster these hopes stirred the masses, who began voicing demands for better economic, social, and religious conditions.

A third stream was the eschatological Anabaptism of Melchior Hoffman (1495–1543), who was one of the most influential disseminators of Anabaptism in northern Europe. A classic traveling preacher and revolutionary on the run, Hoffman was on the move both theologically and physically. Theologically he moved from a passionate support of Lutheran theology (for a time he had Luther's backing) through to more radical views. Physically he was constantly on the hop, received with favor and expelled under suspicion from many places across northern Germany, Friesland, Denmark, Holstein, and Sweden. On the way he built up a swathe of supporters, especially in the Low Countries. Eventually he was thrown behind bars in Strasbourg in 1533, perhaps to fulfill a prophecy he had received a little earlier that his incarceration would speed up the return of the Lord. However, despite the best intentions of his captors, the horsemen of the apocalypse had well and truly bolted. Hoffmann had left his mark on the Dutch baker, firebrand, and prophet Jan Matthys, who hailed from Haarlem. The latter toured the Low Countries, built up quite a following, and then, after some reconnaissance, declared that the nearby city of Münster was the New Jerusalem. He promptly made his way there, arriving on January 5, 1534.

Finally, there was the stream of Reform, which dates back in Münster to the 1520s, when the first waves of the new ideas washed over the city. A distinct leader emerged in the figure of Bernhard Rothmann, a former priest who, after contact with the Reformers in Wittenberg and Strasbourg, returned to Münster to preach the new message. It also helped Rothmann's cause that he managed to win over the support of many of the influential figures and guild leaders in the city. Events moved quickly: Rothmann published a confession of faith; one of the churches (St. Lambert) was occupied on February 18, 1532; all the churches in the city apart from the cathedral became evangelical within six months; and by late 1532 they were joined by Reformers known as the *Wassenberger Prädikanten*. (They hailed from Wassenberg, in the old territory of Jülich, between the Meuse and the Lower Rhine.) With a strong anti–Roman Catholic sentiment and a leaning towards believer's baptism, these Wassenbergers helped divide the Reformers of Münster into two camps: the Lutherans and the more radical Sacramentarian wing, which was open to Anabaptist ideas.

As one would expect with radical social experiments, there was much confusion; events tumbled upon one another; and each day brought a new crisis. Here the historian's often vain desire to string together a coherent narrative faces its greatest test. By early 1534 the struggle for dominance of the town had swung towards the Anabaptists. Visitors (including the colorfully named Bartholomeus Boeckbinder) in January 1534 arrived from the Netherlands and began baptizing adults; the Anabaptists took over the city council and expelled all non-Anabaptists; and the disgruntled and suddenly homeless Roman Catholic bishop, Franz von Waldeck, laid siege to his own see with the help of none other than the Lutherans. The fiery Jan Matthys from Haarlem then turned up and, believing that he was the new Gideon, led a group of thirty out from the walls to raise the siege and to certain death. By August 1534 the lascivious Jan Beukelszoon (van Leyden) declared himself king and immediately took a number of wives, especially in light of the decreasing number of men, and with some struggle a community of goods was established. A betrayer then let a forward party of the besiegers into the city on June 24, 1535, and the leaders—Beukelszoon and a couple of other key figures—were brutally tortured, finally killed, and placed in cages on the steeple of St. Lambert's Church as a warning. The ousted Roman Catholic bishop cleverly exploited the political situation to the full, turning Münster back into a Roman Catholic city in the wake of the discredited Anabaptist Reformers.

As for me, I have a soft spot for the Münster revolutionaries. It is not merely that they tried to create something very new and that some very good people were involved, even if the whole thing unraveled in the end. It is also because the names of some of the key players touch an inchoate and deep familiarity that only the tongue of one's ancestors brings. Bartholomeus Boeckbinder, Wilhem de Cuyper, Jan Matthys, Jan Beukelszoon (van Leyden), and others are distinctly Dutch names. Dutch is the language I first spoke as a child; it can still say things as no other language can; and the Netherlands has a strange and unsettling appeal that keeps me returning. I feel like I know these people at some level, especially since they come from those parts of the Netherlands where Calvinism took root, and there was a great struggle between the Calvinists and the Anabaptists for the allegiance of the common people.

Invariably those who write about the Münster Rebellion cannot help taking sides. Secular scholars, with little sense of how religion affects people in the center of their being "tut-tut," describe the whole business as extreme and "bizarre" (see Howard 1993). Those from an Anabaptist background vigorously distinguish the Münster "aberration" and "catastrophe" from nonviolent Anabaptism, as well as pointing to the way the rebellion was generated out of economic hardship, persecution, and sheer bloody-mindedness of the ruling authorities, whether they were Roman Catholic or Protestant. Ever since, Anabaptists have had to come to terms with what Münster signifies. For their part, Roman Catholics shake their heads with a smug smile as if to say, "I told you so." They see yet another confirmation that the whole Reformation was a wild, lawless, and heretical rebellion against God and pope. At the time, they exploited the situation to the full. By contrast, Protestants nervously wag their finger in disapproval. For Protestants, too, the Anabaptist insurrection in Münster was heretical and sinful, but they were a little more nervous about the whole thing. As if to shore up their argument that the radicals misinterpreted and distorted the Protestant message, the Protestant rulers were as vigorous in suppressing the Anabaptists as their Roman Catholic counterparts.

This is exactly where Calvin found himself when addressing Francis I. Those who had the ear of the king made the most of the situation: "He's no different from that placard wielder who managed to get to your bedroom door, your highness, or those rabid fanatics at Münster, your greatness." In the same way that Roman Catholic *and* Protestant authorities blurred the differences between nonviolent and violent Anabaptists, so also the Roman Catholics asserted that there was little difference between the insurrectionists and Reformers like Calvin. In effect, Calvin had to distinguish himself sharply from the rebels at Münster or the poster makers of Paris. At times he did so quite directly, pointing out that the "disagreements and dogmatic contentions" brought about by those Anabaptists and other "monstrous rascals" were actually the handiwork of Satan (LCC 1:28; OS 3:26.33–27.29). Again and again throughout the *Institutes,* Calvin mentions the misinterpretations of the Anabaptist radicals as something to be avoided at all costs (see *Inst.* 1.9.1; 2.8.26; 2.10.1; 3.3.14; 4.1.13; 4.12.12; 4.16.10–32).

Thomas Müntzer and the Peasants' Revolt

These two events—the Affair of the Placards of 1534 and the concurrent Münster Revolution—served as all-too-vivid reminders of the event that scared the living daylight out of the "Old Corruption" of Europe: the Peasants' Revolt of 1525. When I first became interested in the Peasants' Revolt, I quickly gained an image of a rabble of poor peasants, an angry mob or two ransacking parts of central Europe. To be sure, there was enough of that, but soon I became aware of how extensive the revolt was, how well-trained the peasant armies were, and how it took a concerted effort of deception, intrigue, and military might by the nobility and clergy to crush the peasants. That awareness came when I read one of Friedrich Engels's most famous pieces, "The Peasant War in Germany" ([1850] 1960; [1850] 1978). Or rather, it came when I perused the detailed and lovingly created maps that depicted the various movements of the peasant armies and those of the nobility, the major battles, the towns taken, and the areas under peasant control. They are based on the maps Engels originally drew, which were then re-created in the *Collected Works* in full color and great detail. Someone at Progress Publishers in Moscow—the publisher of the magisterial fifty-volume English collection of Marx's and Engels's works—obviously took much delight in these maps. They made it perfectly clear that the Peasants' Revolt was a major campaign aimed at overthrowing the nobility and the feudal order of society, politics, and economics. It extended across most of the southern regions that eventually became parts of Germany, Austria, and later Italy. And it took all that the nobles, the Roman Catholics, and the Lutherans had to overcome the revolt.

But why in the world would Calvin seek to distance himself from the Peasants' Revolt? One of its main ideologues, inspirations, and instigators was none other than the theologian and reforming firebrand Thomas Müntzer (c. 1489 to May 27, 1525). An outline of Müntzer's brief but eventful career will soon make it clear why a ruler such as Francis I would be dead scared of anyone like Müntzer and why Calvin would desperately seek to distance himself from such a figure.

As a taste of what Müntzer was like, here he is in the *Prague Manifesto* from 1521:

> O ho, how ripe the rotten apples are! O ho, how rotten the elect have become! The time of harvest has come! That is why he himself has hired me for his harvest. I have sharpened my sickle, for my thoughts yearn for the truth and with my lips, skin, hands, hair, soul, body and life I call down curses on unbelievers. . . . Help me for the sake of the blood of Christ to fight against these high enemies of the faith. I will confound them before your very eyes in the spirit of Elijah. For the new apostolic church will start in your land and then spread everywhere.
>
> (Müntzer 1988, 371)

By this time Müntzer was a fully fledged revolutionary. In order to understand how Müntzer became a militant and radical, we need to go back to Müntzer's life-changing time with Luther. Up until this point he had a rather conventional early life. Born in the village of Stolberg around 1489 in the Thuringia region of what eventually became central Germany, he studied for a master's degree in biblical studies on his way to the priesthood. At about twenty-four years of age he was ordained. Yet the life-changing moment was still to come: between 1517 and 1519 he was in Wittenberg, where he met Luther and heard his denunciations of the Church and its practices. Luther's criticisms of priestly graft and worldliness struck to the core of Müntzer's being.

The problem for Müntzer was that Luther did not go far enough. He wanted no half measures, and so he took these criticisms much further than Luther. Indeed, as Müntzer became more of a revolutionary, Luther began to show his cautious and conservative side. Müntzer found himself on an increasingly radical path, feeling himself led forward by his readings of the Bible and the spirit of God speaking directly to him. Luther, on the other hand, felt that Müntzer was straying further from the truth—a crackpot who just went too far. Luther had initially recommended that Müntzer take up the parish of Zwickau in 1520. He soon changed his mind and did his best to have him expelled. Within a year, Müntzer was on the road that led to Prague, where he barely lasted six months, until Christmas in 1521. By this time he was a fully fledged apocalyptic and revolutionary thinker and activist—if the *Prague Manifesto* (Müntzer 1988, 357–79) is anything to go by. Having picked up Luther's main points, he soon left those reforms far behind.

Müntzer was really a professional revolutionary: perpetually on the run and avoiding arrest, plotting against the authorities, writing furiously, organizing followers, seeking out the possibility of yet another coup. While all this was going on, he managed to maintain a voluminous correspondence and write a highly creative and original liturgy (the first in German) as well as texts such as *Counterfeit Faith* and *Protestation or Proposition*, among many others.[6]

Luther thought it high time to step in and put an end to Müntzer's insurrectionary activities. After Müntzer refused an invitation from Luther to meet privately, Luther attacked him publicly in his *Letter to the Princes* (July 1524), a direct counter to Müntzer's earlier *Sermon to the Princes*.[7] Müntzer replied with his *Vindication and Refutation* (1988, 327–50) and gave Luther both barrels. Drawing deeply on the Bible, he called Luther a wily black crow; a boasting, venal, and wily fox; a "Doctor Liar." At Luther's urging, Duke John of Saxony closed Müntzer's propaganda machine (the printing press in Allstedt) and called Müntzer to a hearing. Müntzer refused to appear and instead attempted a coup in Mühlhausen in mid-1524, which at first failed and then succeeded for a few months in early 1525. This was the famous "Eternal League of God," established by popular election from the citizens of the city and based on God's justice, the removal of those with power and wealth, and the exercise of justice by and for the poor, as outlined in the revolutionary Mühlhausen Articles. "In this whole matter," he wrote, "we want action taken without vacillation, without any delay, and in accordance with the word of God" (Müntzer 1988, 458). Soon afterwards, Müntzer would lead his peasant army to their gruesome end at the battle of Frankhausen on May 15, 1525.

At that fateful battle, eight thousand peasants had lined up with Müntzer, expecting God to intervene and inaugurate the kingdom that "shall stand forever" (as Dan. 2:44 would have it). Standing in their way was the small problem of the heavy artillery and trained foot sol-

---

6. See the collection of Müntzer's writings edited and translated by Peter Matheson (Müntzer 1988).

7. Here is a sample from those sermons: "What a pretty spectacle we have before us now—all the eels and snakes coupling together immorally in one great heap! The priests and all the evil clerics are the snakes, as John, who baptised Jesus, called them, Matthew 3, and the secular lords and rulers are the eels, symbolised by the fishes in Leviticus 11. . . . O, my dear lords, what a fine sight it will be when the Lord whirls his rod of iron among the old pots, Psalm 2" (Müntzer 1988, 244–45). His audience included the two princes of Saxony, and the sermon was delivered in Allstedt on July 13, 1524. They were not impressed.

diers of the princes. The peasants were thoroughly routed; Müntzer literally lost his head on May 27 in Thuringia; his head and body were put on display as a warning to any who would try to emulate him.

Müntzer has had a varied press, to say the least. For some, like Luther, he was a wayward Reformer, a man who distorted and twisted the truth. For many today, he is no better than a hopeless dreamer, impractical prophet, and dangerous terrorist. After all, history is littered with such figures—apocalyptic plotters who call on God to bring on Armageddon only to find that God is not paying attention or has perhaps decided that the time is not right. The problem is that there is a fine line between a villain and a hero, between laughable failure and rousing success. Luther himself walked that fine line and owed much to the Elector of Saxony.

For others, Müntzer is a hero, albeit a little flawed. This hero status is usually accorded on two counts, one theological and the other political. Either Müntzer was a formidable theologian who unfortunately became entangled in politics, or he was an astute politician who had to use theological language. On the theological side, Müntzer's disagreements with Luther become theological disputes and are not political differences. For example, against Luther, Müntzer wanted to abolish infant baptism; he argued that the bread and wine of the Lord's Supper were merely emblems of Christ's sacrifice; and he believed firmly in the "living word of God." In other words, God still spoke directly with human beings, especially through visions and dreams. Indeed, Müntzer felt the Spirit of God running through him; the sign of the true minister or pastor was precisely that God used him as a prophetic vessel. Needless to say, the Roman Catholic priests, Luther, and the other Reformers, theologians, and biblical scholars did not quite measure up—they were no better than pleasure-loving pigs, devilish monks, treacherous parsons, and a pack of devils (much like today). I would have loved to hear Müntzer preach, for he would have been spectacular. I would have been less than enthusiastic about serving in his army, for he was obviously lacking in the necessary tactical skills. And I certainly would not have enjoyed being his partner, since he would have tossed and turned in bed as God talked to him in his sleep.

Müntzer has also been a hero of Marxists and other sundry Lefties. The responsibility for this position lies squarely with Friedrich Engels and his book *The Peasant War in Germany* (1960 [1850]; 1978 [1850]). Others in the Marxist tradition would add some nuance to Engels's argument, especially Karl Kautsky ([1895–97] 1947, 2:7–103;

[1897] 2002) and Ernst Bloch (1969), both of whom studied Müntzer in detail. Apart from his great love of military correspondence and analysis, Engels argues that Müntzer's theological language was merely a cloak for his real political agenda. Müntzer could not help speaking in theological and biblical terms since it was the only language in which the peasants could voice their grievances and was the dominant way of thinking about the world as such. Engels goes on to argue that the more political Müntzer becomes, the closer he comes to atheism. In other words, had Müntzer been able to use more secular and economic terms, he would have expressed the peasants' grievances in those terms. It is a curious argument for at least two reasons: it attempts to discard the central role of theology in Müntzer's thought and action (Engels's unsuccessful efforts to dispense with his own Calvinist background play a role here[8]); it makes him a calculating politician who used theological language for another purpose. If Müntzer had been so clever, he might have lasted a little longer.

I find both approaches mistaken, for we cannot separate the political and theological elements of Müntzer's thought and action so easily. A recurring theme in this book is that the political and theological elements are wound so tightly together that it is difficult to separate them. In Müntzer's case it would destroy his integrity, for his theological positions were political and vice versa. For example, his favorite biblical texts are deeply political—apocalyptic texts like Daniel and Revelation, which promise the obliteration of oppressive powers at God's hand, blasting them off the face of the earth for good. These oppressive rulers include the Pharaoh in Egypt, Ahab the king of Israel, Herod in the New Testament, and even Luther. Over against them is a long line of prophets, a line that runs from Moses through Jesus Christ to Müntzer himself: he too is a prophet denouncing oppression and seeking to overthrow the oppressors.

This theological position is precisely why Francis I of France and Calvin found Müntzer so dangerous. He was certainly no hero for either of them. He was more like an ever-present danger. I can imagine Francis at least breaking out in a nervous sweat every time someone or some event reminded him of Thomas Müntzer. For Calvin, Müntzer was an embarrassment and risk. I have an image of Calvin quietly cursing and damning Müntzer as he wrote this preface to Francis. The reason: Müntzer was simply a biblical revolutionary. As God's agent, Müntzer

---

8. For a detailed discussion of Engels's long and complex relationship with Calvinism and biblical scholarship, see my *Criticism of Earth* (Boer forthcoming b).

set out to "seize the very roots of government, following the command of Christ" (Müntzer 1988, 247). He saw resistance to oppression as the heart of the biblical message. That message was not merely some add-on, a political and social cause for which he found the Bible useful. Rather, the Bible itself mandated that he must, in obedience to God, denounce and overthrow the powers that oppress both spiritually and materially. Müntzer's idea of the eternal kingdom of God comes very close to the description of revolution from Calvin's own pen, the one I quoted at the beginning of this chapter.

THEOLOGY

Exegesis and history have had their say, so now it is the turn of the theologian, who I would hope is modest enough not to assert some grand, synthesizing superiority over the others. The theological possibilities emerge from what I have written concerning exegesis and history. The key question concerns the relationship between someone like Calvin and these other radicals. There seem to be two possibilities: either the thoughts and actions of the placard wielders, rebels of Münster, and Thomas Müntzer are the logical outcome of the Reformers' own thoughts, or they are an aberration and misinterpretation. In other words, these radicals are either on a continuum with the Reformers or not; they speak the same language, or they do not. The first position—logical outcome of Reformers' position—was the favored one pursued by Roman Catholic critics and opponents. They are all of the same ilk, argued these opponents: push Luther or Calvin hard enough, and you'll find them plastering a poster to the bedchamber door of the king of France. The second position—aberration—was the one taken by the Reformers themselves. Luther thundered, and Calvin incisively stated that they were miscreants and wayward thinkers who misread the Bible and distorted what it said. Calvin takes this argument a step or three further by stating that such tumult is the work of Satan, that the radical positions of the Anabaptists were the handiwork of the king of darkness, who had set about to confuse the truth by whatever means he had at hand. Nothing new in all of that, for such positions have been rehearsed a thousand times and more since the Reformation.

So let me approach the question from another angle: Calvin's careful denial. Running through the whole discussion of this chapter is the fact that Calvin's preface addressed to Francis I of France is a denial that his own thought is disruptive or revolutionary. "May you not at all be moved," he writes, "by those vain accusations with which our adversaries are trying to inspire terror in you: that by this new gospel (for so they call it) men strive and seek only after the opportunity for seditions and impunity for all crimes" (LCC 1:30; *OS* 3:29.3–7). Instead, Müntzer argues, it is a faithful explanation of what the Bible says. As we will see, he goes on to make regular comments about those who would use the Bible for their own perverted purposes, who would pursue personal dreams of world domination and upset the divine order.

But what is actually going on is the issue of where you draw the line: when does a challenging interpretation of the Bible cross the line to become an aberration? For the Roman Catholics, that line is clear: it is at the boundary of the Church and its authority. In other words, one draws the line early and clearly. Anything beyond that is heresy and misinterpretation—Reformers, Anabaptists, political radicals are all the same. For a Luther or a Calvin, that line is drawn a little further along. Thus their own interpretation is a faithful one, divinely sanctioned by the Bible, but the radical Reformers have stepped over the line and gone off the rails. It matters little whether they are peaceful or violent apocalyptic types, for they are all the same. (I should add the complicating factor that the Reformers also argued that the Roman Catholics were an aberration.) However, for the radical Reformers, that line is further along still. Thus the Anabaptists have long debated the connections between their peaceful and nonviolent wing and the apocalyptic harbingers of the kingdom of God. For the nonviolent types, the line is drawn between them as legitimate interpreters of the Bible and their wayward violent cousins, who are past the line.

But note what has happened: in each case the line is drawn between groups. The Roman Catholics see themselves separate from those wayward Reformers; the Reformers distinguish themselves from both the Roman Catholics, who have lost the way, and the radical Reformers, who have gone too far; the radical Reformers feel that the Reformers have sold out and become no better than the Roman Catholics, but that their violent brethren have gone too far. What if it is not a question of a distinction between groups, between the proverbial us and them, but rather a tension within? In other words, what if the line is drawn not between me and my enemy but within my own group of fellow believers, or even within me? If we do this, the line between faithfulness and unfaithfulness, between true interpretation and aberration, or even between the elect and the damned becomes an internal tension or contradiction. All too often we find that someone takes an internal tension, identifies what he or she feels is "bad" about it, and projects all these negative elements onto someone else. Parents do it with the various character traits in their children—she must get her temper from you, but her brains from me. We do it with personal enemies, opposition football teams, annoying workmates, and so on. So, rather than taking these various scapegoats at face value, I would rather explore the tension within.

This internal contradiction may take a number of forms, but my main interest is the tension between reform and revolution in Calvin's own thought. By now the point should be obvious: less a difference between groups, the tension is one that runs within Calvin himself. It is a classic distinction: reformers wish to tinker with the system in order to make it work better while revolutionaries want to do away with the system and replace it with another. We may frame the tension in different ways, such as that between conservatism and radicalism, reaction and revolution, or indeed trace the way such a tension shows different faces in different contexts. It will have theological, exegetical, social, and political faces, at least to begin with. But it is crucial to understanding what Calvin sought to do.

Let me sum up my argument. Calvin depicts in colorful detail what the charges are against him and his ilk—he wishes to depose kings, cast down lawcourts, annul laws, disrupt the peace and order of society, overthrow the traditions of rank and privilege—in short, turn everything topsy-turvy. While denying this charge, he provides a wonderful description of revolution *and* makes a crucial connection between theology and politics. My theology, he says, or rather the theological message of the Bible, may have political consequences, but not these radical ones. However, after setting his denials to Francis I in the context of the Affair of the Placards, the Münster Revolution, and the Peasants' Revolt, I have argued that the tension between reform and revolution or between conservatism and radicalism is not found merely between groups. It is also found within. Calvin may say that "we" are not like "them," but there is an element of "them" in his own thought. In other words, Calvin is not an all-out revolutionary (we can accept his denials to some extent), but he is not a conservative either (the charges of his opponents have a grain of truth in them). His thought struggles between these poles.

2
Bible

The Irrepressible Book

Mention Calvin and the Bible in one breath, and the words that jump to mind are "conservative" and even "infallible." While there are elements within Calvin's texts that point in this direction, these labels miss the point. "Conservative" is not really the best word here: "high" is much better. In short, Calvin has a high rather than a conservative view of Scripture, and that high view has revolutionary potential.

My argument has three points. To begin with, Calvin asserts that the Bible is beholden to no earthly authority, especially the Church. In order to achieve this move, he attempts to raise the Bible above grasping human hands. When it has achieved such a dizzying height, Calvin explores a number of overlapping features of this elevated Bible: it is self-sufficient, but then it also comes from God's mouth, and the way we know that it is God's word is by the testimony of the Holy Spirit. Finally, this high position leads in two directions, one conservative and the other far more radical. Conservatively, one must never question the Bible, for it comes from God (Calvin spends a good deal of time countering criticism of the Bible). More radically, it means that one's faith and hopes rest with no earthly person. If that text exhorts one to pursue revolutionary politics, then you had better do so.

OUT OF THE REACH OF HUMAN HANDS

The initial move in Calvin's discussion of the Bible comes swiftly:

> It is utterly vain, then, to pretend that the power of judging Scripture so lies with the church that its certainty depends upon her nod.
> (*Inst.* 1.7.2; translation modified)

> *Vanissimum est igitur commentum, Scripturae iudicandae potestatem esse penes Ecclesiam: ut ab huius nutu illius certitudo pendere intelligatur.*
> (*OS* 3:66.27–29)

There are no qualifications or padded introductions: *vanissimum* is promoted to the beginning of the sentence. It is the superlative form of the adjective *vanus*, meaning the emptiest, the most vain, groundless, and false. If we translate closer to the Latin syntax, the sentence begins, "Most absurd it is therefore . . ." What is the most absurd or empty? It is the claim that the Church has the power of judging Scripture (*Scripturae iudicandae potestatem*). Or more graphically, the claim that "upon her nod" (*ab huius nutu*) does certitude hang.

Calvin expends a great deal of ammunition attacking the Church's assumptions that it holds not merely the keys of heaven and hell but also the key to the Bible. Here he lets loose with less economy:

> But a most pernicious error widely prevails that Scripture has only so much weight as is conceded to it by the consent of the church. As if the eternal and inviolable truth of God depended upon the decision of men [*hominem arbitrio niteretur*]! For they mock the Holy Spirit when they ask: Who can convince us that these writings came from God? Who can assure us that Scripture has come down whole and intact even to our very day? Who can persuade us to receive one book in reverence but to exclude another, unless the church prescribe a sure rule for all these matters? What reverence is due Scripture and what books ought to be reckoned within its canon depend, they say, upon the determination of the church.
> (*Inst.* 1.7.1; *OS* 3:65.19–66.4)

If it weren't for the Church, so the argument went and still goes, the Bible would not exist. After all, did not the Church in its early days decide on the ins and the outs—what was to be included within and excluded from the canon? Even more, does not the Church guarantee that the Bible has passed down safely and without error until now? And is it not the Church who can assure us that the Bible does in fact come from God? By the end of this quoted text, these three arguments become two: the reverence due to Scripture and the nature of the canon, both of which depend on the Church.

For Calvin, all of this is anathema, or as he puts it, a most pernicious error and an insult to the Holy Spirit.[1] The point at issue is that this whole position assumes that "the eternal and inviolable truth of God depended upon the decision of men." I will come back to this point in a moment, but first let me pick up one feature of this text. Calvin challenges the argument that the Church determined which books are to be included in the canon. He conjures up an image of the Church sitting down before a vast pile of books, placing one carefully in a box with "canon" emblazoned on its outside and tossing another into a large bin called "rejects." Such an image leads to outrage that anyone should determine what the word of God might be. Unfortunately, the vast majority of opinion concerning the formation of the canon would place Calvin in a distinct minority.[2] The long, slow process of canonical formation, the debates over books such as Esther, Song of Songs, *The Shepherd of Hermas*, and Hebrews; the political struggles; influence of Constantine and later Roman emperors; late closure (in the fourth century if it is indeed closed today)—all of these point to a very human process. In light of this data, the Roman Catholics were wrong as well, for it was not merely the Church in its divine wisdom that decided on the canon. All manner of extra-ecclesial factors played their roles as well, not least the "Christian" emperors keen on ideological cohesion among their religious backers. In the end it seems that Calvin was wrong on this point, but then so were his opponents in the Roman Catholic Church. And for those who would insist that it is wrong to impose judgments from the twenty-first century onto the sixteenth, it is worth remembering that there are a good many who hold to Calvin's position as I write.

In the end I am not so interested in whether Calvin is right or wrong on these matters. Far more interesting is why he should make such

---

1. I must admit I would love to use such a phrase in an argument: that is a most pernicious error and an insult to the Holy Spirit.
2. As a small sample of key texts on canonization, see Sundberg (1964), Brettler (1994), Carr (1996), Davies (1998), and Aichele (2001). The status of the debate and all the key positions are covered in McDonald and Sanders (2002). With a bird's eye view, these debates oscillate within three oppositions: diversity versus unity, conflict versus consensus, and rupture versus organic or evolutionary development. If you begin from the side of unity and consensus, then the problems arise with diversity and conflict, and vice versa. Often such reconstructions come up with ingenious and overlapping combinations of these three oppositions, with, for instance, an organic development broken by a rupture or two, or a consensus as the resolution of conflict, or a final unity out of diversity that is yet plagued by diversity. The dates vary between the supposed time of Ezra and Nehemiah (sixth century BCE), through the era of the Hasmoneans (second to first century BCE), to the rabbinic efforts in the first centuries of the Common Era. As any historian worth his or her salt knows, dates in scholarship are like the fashion in skirts: they go either up or down.

a move. Initially he wants to negate the argument from the Roman Catholic Church that the Bible depends on the decisions of the Church and that its correct interpretation is therefore in the Church's hands. This much is well known. But Calvin goes much further: the Bible cannot and should not "depend on the decision of men [*hominem arbitrio niteretur*]." *Arbitrium* has a stronger semantic cluster than what is conveyed by "decision"; it has the sense of judgment, mastery, and dominion. So Calvin is saying that the Bible should not depend on the mastery and dominion of men. He wants to remove the Bible not merely from the clutches of the Church but also from the greasy fingers of any human being—and that should include Calvin himself.

At this point his position on Scripture locks into his theological system as a whole. No human being—sinful, fallen, and depraved as we are—can or should be able to tell God to do anything. Salvation depends purely on God's grace through Christ; no one can deny or accept God through his or her own power; even faith is a gift from God and not a human capacity or faculty. So also with the Bible: since all have sinned and fallen short of the glory of God, it is hands off.

At this point Calvin betrays his deep knowledge of classical philosophy,[3] even though he tries to align himself with Paul and distance himself from the wisdom of this world. In particular he draws on Augustine, who in turn draws on Plato's still-useful distinction between opinion and truth (*doxa* and *alēthē*) (*Inst.* 1.7.3; OS 3:68.26–27). Opinion is all too easy and cheap, argues Plato, but truth is very difficult to find. When I occasionally peruse the opinion pages of the newspaper or sit at a table full of people, I soon find that opinion is indeed cheap. Anyone can spout it forth to the great enlightenment of those around. But truth, a genuine gem, is a difficult business indeed. Here Calvin uses the distinction in regard to the Bible: the mere opinion of human beings concerning the Bible is not something to which we should pay too much attention. Rather, what we seek is the truth.

THE CHICKEN AND THE EGG, AUTO-FAITH, GOD AND THE HOLY SPIRIT

So far I have dealt only with a negative argument: Calvin wishes to deny the Church control of the Bible and thereby block any human

---

3. This is the starting assumption of Paul Helm's useful study, *John Calvin's Ideas* (2004): for all Calvin's championing of antiphilosophy in the name of divine "foolishness," he makes use of philosophical arguments and assumptions where necessary.

being from interfering with it. He also launches a series of positive arguments: what I call the chicken-and-the-egg argument; the self-sufficiency of the Bible or what may be named "auto-faith"; the mouth-of-God argument; the witness-of-the-Holy-Spirit position. While Calvin manages to weave these arguments into a loose logical whole, they also raise deep problems for his argument. Let us explore them one at a time.

Step One: Chicken and Egg

The first of these is much like the conundrum of the chicken and the egg. What came first: the Bible or the Church? Neither answer is satisfying. If one says, "The Church," then the question we must ask is how the Church came about. If one then answers that the Church arose because of the Bible, then we are in exactly the same position, albeit in reverse. Calvin's solution is disarmingly simple:

> But such wranglers are neatly refuted by just one word of the apostle. He testifies that the church is "built upon the foundation of the prophets and apostles" [Eph. 2:20]. If the teaching of the prophets and apostles is the foundation, this must have had authority before the church began to exist.
> (*Inst.* 1.7.2; *OS* 3:66.16–20)

It is not the Bible itself that came first but those who wrote it. The apostles and the prophets were divinely inspired, acting as God's scribes, and so their unique status gives the Bible its sacred status. So the answer to our question is that neither the Bible nor the Church came first, but the prophets and apostles who wrote that text in the first place. The problem with such an argument is that it doesn't solve the problem entirely. Are not the apostles the first signs of the Church? If they wrote the Bible under God's direction, does that not mean that the Church is primary? Calvin moves on to the next argument, namely, the self-sufficiency of the Bible.

Step Two: Auto-faith

For this option I would like to pick up an important text, one that will be my focus for the next three steps:

Let this point therefore stand: that those whom the Holy Spirit has inwardly taught truly rest upon Scripture, and that Scripture indeed is self-authenticated; hence, it is not right to subject it to proof and reasoning. And the certainty it deserves with us, it attains by the testimony of the Spirit. For even if it wins reverence for itself by its own majesty, it seriously affects us only when it is sealed upon our hearts through the Spirit. Therefore, illumined by his power, we believe neither by our own nor by anyone else's judgment that Scripture is from God; but above human judgment we affirm with utter certainty (just as if we were gazing upon the majesty of God himself) that it flowed to us from the very mouth of God by the ministry of men.

(*Inst.* 1.7.5)

Maneat ergo hoc fixum, quos Spiritus sanctus intus docuit, solide acquiescere in Scriptura, et hanc quidem esse αὐτόπιστον, neque demonstrationi et rationibus subiici eam fas esse: quam tamen meretur apud nos certitudinem, Spiritus testimonio consequi. Etsi enim reverentiam sua sibi ultro maiestate conciliat, tunc tamen demum serio nos afficit quum per Spiritum obsignata est cordibus nostris. Illius ergo virtute illuminati, iam nos aut nostro, aut aliorum iudicio credimus, a Deo esse Scripturam: sed supra humanum iudicium, certo certius constituimus (non secus acsi ipsius Dei numen illic intueremur) hominem ministerio, ab ipsissimo Dei ore ad nos fluxisse.

(*OS* 3:70.16–27)

This is an extraordinarily good statement of Calvin's position on the Bible, so let us examine it closely. The key word is "self-authenticated," or as Beveridge's translation from 1845 puts it, "carrying its own evidence along with it." These are actually gallant efforts to translate one of the occasional Greek words that turn up in Calvin's text: *autopiston* (αὐτόπιστον). We are familiar with *auto*, for it is a common prefix that means "by itself" or "on its own." An *auto*mobile is a vehicle able to move on its own, without a horse, dog, human being, or other vehicle such as a locomotive. *Auto*matic means that an appliance can operate according to its own devices and does not rely on my hand or finger to get it going—automatic gears on a bicycle, an automatic washing machine, and so on. In Greek, of course, *autos* is the reflexive pronoun, the one that folds back on oneself—or himself, herself, themselves, and the rest. *Piston* is another form of the word *pistis*, meaning faith or belief. So *autopiston* (αὐτόπιστον) means something like "having its belief within itself" (we are talking about the Bible), or "believable on its own" or even "self-sufficient in terms of faith." I prefer the simple "auto-faith": the Bible is an *auto-faith* document.

What does that mean? To begin with, this auto-faith document is not to be subjected to "proofs and arguments [*demonstrationi et rationibus*]." It should not require any external demonstrations or explanations, nor should one need to make any arguments concerning it. It simply bears witness to itself and silences any such debates. At this point Calvin adds an explanation from the 1539 edition (the original edition was from 1536), since he obviously felt his point was not clear enough: "For even if it wins reverence for itself by its own majesty, it seriously affects us only when it is sealed upon our hearts through the Spirit." Here we find that "auto-faith" gains an explanation: the Bible has "its own majesty [*sibi ultro maiestate*]." No one needs to act as its publicity agent, for it does well enough on its own.

Further, the Bible is self-sufficient because it mirrors God: in the same way that God is self-sufficient, so also is the Bible. If God has no need of external support or verification, neither does the Bible. One is *autotelic* (has its own ends within itself) and the other is *auto-faith*. Or as Calvin puts it, "The highest proof of Scripture derives in general from the fact that God in person speaks in it" (*Inst.* 1.7.4; *OS* 3:68.30–69.1).

Step Three: Mouth of God

A high view of Scripture, is it not? The Bible resembles God's nature in more ways than one. Now, at this point Calvin runs the distinct danger of bibliolatry. While he wishes to keep the Bible in the role of being a witness or a sign that points to God, he does show the tendency of making the Bible an idol. Originally a product of human hands, it becomes an object of worship in its own right, especially since it is the only witness to God available to us. Now, while Calvin manages to dig his heels in and stop the slide down that slippery and muddy hillside, his followers have not always been so successful.

Here is Calvin: "It is clear that the teaching of God is from heaven" (*Inst.* 1.7.4; *OS* 69:19–20). Let me add to this the text I quoted earlier: "The highest proof of Scripture derives in general from the fact that God in person speaks in it" (*Inst.* 1.7.4; *OS* 3:68.30–69.1). It is a point he will repeat again and again: the Bible is full of heavenly teaching and thereby reflects the character of God. Why is the Bible so much like God? Why is it self-sufficient, auto-faith, and autotelic? It is not that the Bible is like

God and threatens to replace God, but that Scripture has been spoken by God and therefore contains his own ideas, thoughts, and doctrine.

This text is important for another reason: it throws a line out of a circular argument. The circular argument looks like this: how do we know that the Bible is the word of God? It says so, and therefore we should believe it. That argument is about as persuasive as arguing that I am trustworthy because I say I am. How do you know that I am to be trusted? I have told you so. Most worldly wise people would take such a circular argument *cum grano salis*. Calvin squeezes out of that problem with what is really a grappling iron. The image I have in mind is of Calvin stuck in an alcove, a cul-de-sac from which the known escape routes have been closed. He twirls a rope with a grappling iron on the end, hurls it upward, and it grips a ledge high above. So also with the Bible, at least in Calvin's assessment: the grappling iron thrown out from the self-sufficiency and auto-faith of the Bible latches onto God. In fact, the Bible turns out not to be a self-sufficient, autonomous, and self-verifying text. It is actually dependent on God: it contains the heavenly doctrine, comes from the "very mouth of God," so much so that it is as though "we were gazing upon the majesty of God himself [*ipsius Dei numen illic intueremur*]" (*Inst.* 1.7.5; *OS* 3:70.25–6).

This is an even higher view of Scripture. Firmly gripping the rope attached to the grappling hook, Calvin has hauled the Bible upwards so that it is out of human reach. People may have written it, but they were mere instruments—"by the ministry of men "[*hominem ministerio*]" (*Inst.* 1.7.5; *OS* 3:70.26–27). However, Calvin has created another problem for himself. With such a lofty view of the Bible, the question then becomes How do we really know that it is God's word? It may claim to be so, and we may state that it comes from the mouth of God, but how do we—or rather, how does Calvin—know?

Step Four: Holy Spirit

Once again, the answer is disarmingly simple: the Holy Spirit. Now another building block falls into place from the text I quoted earlier: "Those whom the Holy Spirit has inwardly taught truly rest upon Scripture [*quos Spiritus sanctus intus docuit, solide acquiescere in Scriptura*]" (*Inst.* 1.7.5; *OS* 3:70.16–17). The key words here are *intus*, *solide*, and *acquiescere*. *Intus* designates what is "within" or "on the inside"; in other words, it is that private, personal zone where the Holy Spirit does its teaching. *Solide* has the sense of fully or surely, and *acquiesco* (obviously the basis of acquiesce) means to come to rest and to be satisfied. So the sense of this clause concerns those who are taught on the inside by the Holy Spirit: as a result they come to a full rest and end up being completely satisfied and content with the Bible.[4]

But let us step back a moment and consider the wider context of this clause. It is actually part of an important sentence structure at the beginning of the quotation. The passage actually begins with a main clause: "Let this point therefore stand [*Maneat ergo hoc fixum*]." From there we get two subordinate clauses, one focusing on the teaching and witness of the Holy Spirit and the other on the self-sufficiency of the Bible—both of which are established (*fixum*). It is firmly established, Calvin argues, (1) that those who are inwardly taught (*intus docuit*) by the Holy Spirit acknowledge the authority and power of Scripture, and (2) that the Bible is a self-sufficient and auto-faith document and does not need external proofs or evidence. I have explored the second of these items already so I focus on the first here.[5] Add to this text another one, and the picture starts to clear: "And the certainty it deserves with us, it attains by the testimony of the Spirit [*quam tamen meretur apud nos certitudinem, Spiritus testimonio consequi*]" (*Inst.* 1.7.5; *OS* 3:70.20–21). The Holy Spirit provides certainty or full conviction (*certitudo*) to those who are taught inwardly (*intus docuit*) that the Bible comes from the very mouth of God.

Reading these passages generates a strange sense of déjà vu for me, since I feel as though I am hearing yet again one of those long Bible studies at the youth camps I used to attend many years ago for my sins. There we would be told, especially for doubters and questioners like myself, that the reason we know that the Bible is the (inerrant and infallible) Word of God is because the Holy Spirit tells us within our innermost being. Should we still harbor doubts on this line concerning the Bible, then it was clear that the Holy Spirit was not in fact witnessing to us— given that the Holy Spirit was actually witnessing in the way that our able and serious youth leaders told us he or she was in fact witnessing.

However, a careful reading of Calvin's text at least allows me to make some sense of where these earnest teachers were coming from and where they ran off in the wrong direction. Calvin may have been using

---

4. At this point a contradiction emerges from Calvin's treatment of the Bible: despite asserting that the Holy Spirit is the sole and sufficient verification of the Bible, he also devotes a long chapter to "proving" its age, reliability, and pedigree (see *Inst.* 1.8). It reminds one all too much of the old problem of the genealogies of Jesus: if he is born of the Holy Spirit, then why produce a genealogy at all?

5. Someone may object that I have artificially separated two points that appear side by side in Calvin's text, so I would emphasize that we need to distinguish between logical distinctions and the rhetorical effect of this text. Here we have two distinct ways of dealing with the Bible, which Calvin tries to bring into touch with one another.

the Holy Spirit to back up his own position, especially in this ingenious way (and who hasn't fallen back on a similar use of a higher authority from time to time to give their own position a much needed boost?). Yet the main reason he draws on the Holy Spirit is that he needs to get away from even the faintest whiff of human authority. As he puts it, "Therefore, illumined by his power, we believe *neither by our own nor by anyone else's judgment* that Scripture is from God [*Illius ergo virtute illuminati, iam nos aut nostro, aut aliorum iudicio credimus, a Deo esse Scripturam*]" (*Inst.* 1.7.5; *OS* 3:70.24–25). The key phrase is italicized in the English translation above: neither on our own judgment (*iudicio*) or that of others. It is easy to say that the judgment of others is suspect but that my own is rock solid. Calvin will have none of it: your judgment *and mine* are not to be trusted. Why? It is "human judgment" (*humanum iudicium*), and he is after something superior to (*supra*) that all-too-fallible type of judgment, Calvin's own included.

I would like to throw a spoiler into this line of argument, for Calvin is not always consistent. For one who deprecated his own judgment, he seems to have had a high opinion of his own work. For example, in the "Subject of the Present Work" prefixed to the French edition of the *Institutes* in 1560, he puts down his own abilities and the book "for fear of seeming to appraise my work too highly [*de peur qu'il ne semble que ie prise trop mon ouvrage*]" (*OS* 3:8.3–4; my translation), but then he goes on to claim that it provides *the* key to understanding the Bible. Warming to his theme, he lays his cards on the table: the *Institutes* are really "God's more than mine" (LCC 1:8; *OS* 3:8.15). When I first read these words, I laughed. What presumption, claiming that what one has written is actually God's work and therefore everyone should read it and memorize it (a task and half at that) as a sure guide to Scripture. But it is actually a rather clever move. The secret to it is his belief that the *Institutes* contain truth and sound doctrine, and the only way they can do so is through the Holy Spirit. If that is the case, then the book must be the work of God. While we may point out that this is a rather convenient way of avoiding saying "because I said so," I suspect Calvin actually believed that God spoke through him.

The Bible Model

With this underlying drive to remove the Bible from human hands, we come full circle. So I would like to close with a diagram that links these various steps together in the coherent whole that Calvin seeks. I began with Calvin's argument that the authors of the Bible, the apostles and the prophets, are actually the ones responsible for its high status. In order to close down objections to this argument (that the apostles actually constitute the first church), Calvin suggests that we have an auto-faith Bible and asserts that it comes from the mouth of God and that we know through the witness of the God, who

↑
is author of
↓
the auto-faith Bible,
↑
which is witnessed to by
the Holy Spirit, who gives the link with
↓
human beings, who have no authority over the Bible.

The image that keeps coming to mind is either of a pyramid . . .

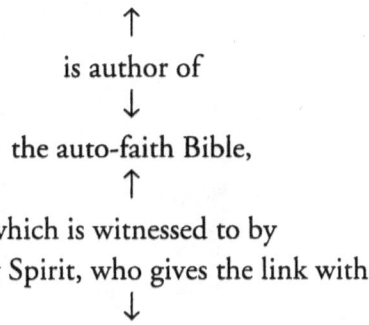

... or of a balloon: the basket or compartment for passengers is the Bible, which the balloon itself tries to lift off the ground and out of human reach. Preventing God and the Bible from disappearing into the clouds is a rope that ties the whole contraption to a stake in the ground. This line is surely the Holy Spirit, who provides that vital link between the passenger compartment (Bible) and people on the ground.

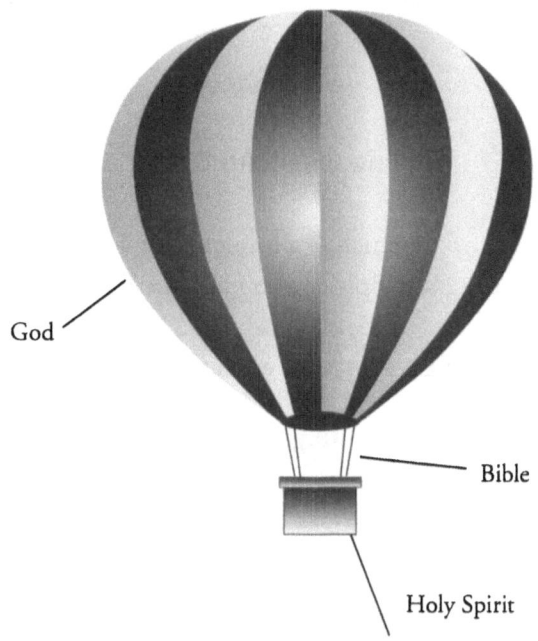

CONSERVATIVES AND RADICALS ON THE HIGH GROUND

Calvin's view of the Bible, or doctrine of Scripture, as the more orthodox would have it, is a very high one. It may well be much higher, drifting off into the clouds, were it not for the Holy Spirit, whose task is to remind the Bible that it is actually written for human beings and to verify to those same human beings that it is nothing less than the voice of God. This position also has more than a trace of Christology about it: replace the Bible with Christ, one Word for another Word, and we have a form of the Trinitarian relationship. Christ becomes the point of tension, like the Bible, between heaven and earth, between God and human beings. We even have a role for the Holy Spirit, who ensures that the Christ of the ascension maintains his links with the earth he has recently left below him.

Now, two paths lead from this high view of the Bible. One is distinctly conservative and the other more radical. One is well trodden, so much so that over the years it became a distinct track through the forest. Eventually picks and shovels were brought in, trees felled, passes and culverts and bridges constructed, stone and bitumen laid. Still the traffic increased, so the road was widened from one lane to two and then to four. Food and fuel outlets became established along the road so that travelers could stop, fuel up their vehicles and bodies with equally fast forms of energy, and get under way as quickly as possible.

This path is of course the conservative one. A great pile of statements seem to stack up on the side of such a conservative direction: "Scripture is from God [*a Deo esse Scripturam*]," writes Calvin (*Inst.* 1.7.5; *OS* 3:70.26); the Bible "flowed to us from the very mouth of God by the ministry of men [*hominem ministerio, ab ipsissimo Dei ore ad nos fluxisse*]" (*Inst.* 1.7.5; *OS* 3:70.26–7); since "there are manifest signs of God speaking in Scripture," it is thus "clear that the teaching of God is from heaven" (*Inst.* 1.7.4; *OS* 69:18–20). From God, from the very mouth of God, spoken by God—the statements couldn't be more direct or clearer.

I could go on, listing such statements endlessly, although I will allow myself a couple more where Calvin lets his literary imagination run loose. So we find that in the Bible we gaze "upon the majesty of God himself [*ipsius Dei numen*]" (*Inst.* 1.7.5; *OS* 3:70.25). Or in this wonderful if somewhat pagan evocation of the Minotaur's labyrinth in *Jason and the Argonauts,* the Bible becomes Ariadne's thread: "For we should so reason that the splendor of the divine countenance, which even the apostle calls 'unapproachable' [1 Tim. 6:16], is for us like an inexplicable labyrinth unless we are conducted into it by the thread of the Word" (*Inst.* 1.6.3; *OS* 3:63.31–64.2).[6]

---

6. And then there is this great text: "Just as old or bleary-eyed men and those with weak vision, if you thrust before them a most beautiful volume, even if they recognize it to be some sort of writing, yet can scarcely construe two words, but with the aid of spectacles will begin to read distinctly; so Scripture, gathering up the otherwise confused knowledge of God in our minds, having dispersed our dullness, clearly shows us the true God. This, therefore, is a special gift, where God, to instruct the church, not merely uses mute teachers but also opens his own most hallowed lips. Not only does he teach the elect to look upon a god, but also shows himself as the God upon whom they are to look" (*Inst.* 1.6.1; *OS* 3:60.25–61.4). I have quoted this text because it is a little close to home. What Calvin describes as being scarcely able to "construe two words" is now known as presbyopia—old person's blindness, or more strictly, the inability of the eyes to focus at close range as one gets a little older. Less than a year ago I found that I too had presbyopia and am now "with the aid of spectacles" able "to read distinctly."

All of these statements about the Bible's proceeding from the hand or mouth of God, providing true doctrine and clear teaching, may well give the impression that Calvin is a deeply conservative theologian. Without a doubt, one part of him is. We need only take all of the preceding statements and link them in with a comment like the following to land in the lap of the fundamentalists (or conservative evangelicals, as some like to call themselves): "It is not right to subject it to proofs and reasonings [*neque demonstrationi et rationibus subiici eam fas esse*]."

The Bible does not submit to proofs and reasonings (*demonstrationi et rationibus*), or, to fill out the semantic field of the Latin, to descriptions, expositions, and judgments. I would like to stay with this comment for a few moments. To begin with, its target is the Roman Catholic claim that the Church is the arbiter of the canon, its interpretation, and the faithful transmission of the Bible. I have already covered Calvin's challenge to the Church at the beginning of this chapter, as well as the more comprehensive step in which no human judgment, proof, or argument whatsoever is needed to verify the Bible as the Word of God. But there are also other targets. Calvin never misses the opportunity to take swipes at critics of the Bible both inside and outside the Church. These may be the Donatists, Pelagians, or Manicheans who populate Augustine's texts (Calvin sometimes seems to think of himself as Augustine redivivus), or the Anabaptists and other radical interpreters of his own day, or the scholars who question the authenticity of biblical books (*Inst.* 1.8.10; *OS* 3:78.16–33), especially Moses' authorship of the Pentateuch or even that Moses existed at all (see *Inst.* 1.8.9; *OS* 3:77.26–35).[7] And where do all these critics get their ammunition? From Satan, of course (*Inst.* 1.8.12; *OS* 3:80.20–26).

Another target emerged well after Calvin, although its seeds were emerging with the intermittent work of Thomas Hobbes ([1651] 1962), Benedict de Spinoza ([1670] 1951) and Jean Astruc, an eighteenth-century author of not only the first great treatise on syphilis but of a small anonymous and critical book on the Bible called *Conjectures sur la Genèse* (Astruc 1999). I am speaking of the historical-critical approach to the Bible, an approach that came into its own in nineteenth-century German scholarship and then became orthodoxy for biblical scholars in the first three-quarters of the twentieth century.

---

7. Calvin's suggested treatment of such scholars is a practice we have lost: "Yet if anyone were to call in doubt whether there ever was a Plato, an Aristotle, or a Cicero, who would not say that such folly ought to be chastised with the fist or the lash?" (*Inst.* 1.8.9; *OS* 3:77.31–33). Conferences would certainly be much livelier if we introduced that practice!

With its basic agenda being the search for the literary history of the texts that make up the Bible and the history behind those texts, historical criticism worked with the basic assumption that research on the Bible should operate with the removal of God from the scene. This was the basic requirement for a "scientific" discipline of biblical studies. Like any other scientific discipline, historical-biblical criticism sought to remove the divine postulate. All too often historical critics were kidding themselves, for they lived dual lives: in one they were purely scientific scholars, and in another they attended church or synagogue on the weekend, often with leadership roles.

For many who call themselves Calvinists, historical criticism was and is highly problematic. The problems were and are many: the removal of God as a factor in biblical criticism; the challenges to traditional views of authorship and provenance; and the use of reason ("proofs and reasonings") as the prime criterion for biblical criticism. All of these go against the basic theological assumption that sinful and fallen human beings should not dare to criticize the Bible. To offer human arguments, human constructs, and human criticisms of the Bible was the ultimate hubris. If the Bible gives us the thread through the mind of God, if it is the utterance from the very mouth of God and spouts forth divine doctrines, then human beings should accept it as it is and not question or criticize.

I know this conservative reading of Calvin all too well. Apart from buttressing it with the doctrine of the inerrancy of the Bible, all manner of twisting and turning goes on to justify that Moses did indeed write the Pentateuch; that Luke did write the third Gospel and Acts; that Paul wrote Colossians, Ephesians, and the letters to Timothy; that Isaiah was written by one person who predicted many things; that the Gospels are eyewitness accounts; that the narratives we find in the Bible are historically accurate. . . . On and on it goes, using the defense that one should not criticize the Word of God and that these positions have the weight of two thousand years behind them.[8]

This conservative reading is one path that may lead on from Calvin's high doctrine of Scripture. But there is another path that is far less traveled. It reminds me of a long twenty-five-kilometer (15.5-mile) walk I undertook some thirty years ago in Lamington National Park in the Great Dividing Range of eastern Australia. After plunging deep into the rain forest and fending off enough leeches to suck an elephant dry,

---

8. This odd claim, very common when historical criticism was first making inroads, has come back into vogue. I have heard my father use it, as well as a reviewer of my *Rescuing the Bible* (Boer 2007c), and Frances Watson.

I found that the trail joined an old bullock team track. Often it disappeared at river crossings, and I struggled to find it again, or it would be buried under a massive fallen tree and its attendant vines and branches. It had been quite a while since anyone had been on this track, for in many places the undergrowth had established itself again, and the leaves made it appear like any other part of the bush. Only the faintest suggestion of a gradient or a cutting kept me on the path. And then that tree root over which I was about to step would move, and a carpet snake would slowly rise to see who was disturbing its quiet sunbathing. As a smallish constrictor, they are relatively harmless, but in a country that has the nine most deadly snakes in the world, one grows up being cautious of our blessed serpent friends. Eventually I found my way back to the campsite on this unbeaten track.

The radical possibilities of Calvin's high view of Scripture are like this path: less well traveled, often concealed, disappearing at crucial moments, and full of deterrents. Yet the track is there; it just takes a little more work to follow it. Calvin's position—that the Bible is God's word alone, coming from the mouth of God, and not due to any human decision or control—is a risky line to take. Even the point of contact between human beings and the Bible is very much a one-way affair: the Holy Spirit witnesses to us that it is God's word; we do not twist the Holy Spirit's arm, mutter a threat, and try to get it to persuade God of our opinion.

If we take Calvin at his word and assume (as most do) that he is in deadly earnest, this position is risky on at least three counts: (1) it gives God free rein to say what God will; (2) it means that we are utterly dependent on the Bible for direction; and (3) the Bible may well upset and overturn any human efforts. I suspect that Calvin sensed the radical possibility of these assumptions—there is enough in his work to suggest that he did. So, while we find him saying often enough that people should be able to read the plain sense of Scripture, he says even more often that the ordinary reader needs a guide for the Bible. It is not difficult to guess what that guide is. For example, he writes of those who spend their whole lives tangling up the "simplicity of Scripture" (LCC 1:22; OS 3:22.6) with all manner of subtleties, dialectical twists, endless disputes, and speculation. I must confess that I always think of a biblical studies conference when I read these words or of those professional biblical scholars who are my colleagues and friends. None of that, says Calvin: let us keep the simplicity of the Bible. If the Bible speaks the mind of God, uttered through his mouth to those who wrote it, then we must take what God says without applying some test of reason or correct doctrine or church interpretation, for these are all the acts of human beings.

Yet Calvin asserts time and again that we really need a good guide to the Bible. So he says that even though the Bible is complete and perfect in itself, to which nothing can be added, "yet a person who has not much practice in it has good reason for some guidance and direction" (LCC 1:6; *OS* 3:7.22–23) so that we may follow the right path. He goes on to state that a key to understanding the Bible is nothing less than his own *Institutes*, which all should memorize as an indispensable guide. And so we have a massive work, whose sole purpose is to help us understand the Bible properly. Once Calvin has set an example, we then find a host of others telling how to read Calvin: one sets out to show how Calvin's *Institutes* follows the steps of the ancient creed; another provides one hundred aphorisms to sum up the work; yet another an introduction. . . . As far as Calvin is concerned, I suspect that he did not quite trust the ordinary reader and the simple truth of Scripture, for there is far too much political gunpowder in that text.

For instance, when the Bible offers a stinging rebuke of economic injustice and oppression, then Calvin should take notice. The words of Isaiah or Micah or Amos are well known for their condemnations of economic exploitation and the oppression of the poor by the powerful rich. There are not a few words placed in the mouth of Jesus that flow in a similar direction. Or when the Bible offers visions of collective living in places such as the Acts of the Apostles or the Gospels, where everyone has all things in common, then we should pay attention. No matter how visionary or even mythical such pictures may be, they have given and continue to give political traction to religious and not-so-religious radicals. Or when we find that the Bible offers narratives of inclusion rather than exclusion, of openness rather than closure (as with the story of Peter's dream in Acts 10:9–16), then we ignore them at our peril. Or indeed when we come across hints of the celebration of chaos and rebellion over against the imposition of order and control, then we should celebrate and rejoice in them. I will return to each of these themes in the conclusion.

3
Grace

The Question of Revolution

My interest in this chapter is grace, *gratia* in Latin, *charis* in Greek. The argument may be stated simply: Calvin glimpses the radical possibilities of grace only to try to contain it. A little more fully, the militant revolutionary potential for grace shows up in a direct ratio with depravity. The more Calvin argues for our utter sinfulness, the more radical grace becomes. The greater the extent of our depraved and corrupt state, the greater becomes the task for grace. But then, just when Calvin pronounces a thoroughly transformative and re-creative role for grace, he steps in and tries to limit grace. He sets about stipulating in a careful and ordered fashion what grace can and cannot do so that eventually it is tamed and limited. This is where our friend the cat gains a real sight of daylight. Calvin gives him a good glimpse, but just as he is about to leap forth into freedom, Calvin clamps the mouth of the bag tightly shut.

LETTING GRACE HAVE ITS HEAD

Grace appears in Calvin's work as the bedrock for the great themes of providence, election, justification by faith (and not works), redemption, and sanctification. To be completely reliant on God for salvation is to rely entirely on his grace. But I do not wish to trot out conventional Calvinist phrases and terms as though I were at some catechism class. Rather, as in the previous chapters, I much prefer to begin with a quotation from Calvin, this time concerning grace:

> Since willing and doing take their origin from faith, we ought to see what is the source of faith itself. But since the whole of Scripture proclaims that faith is a free gift of God, it follows that when we, who are by nature inclined to evil with our whole heart, begin to will good, we do so out of mere grace. Therefore, the Lord when he lays down these two principles in the conversion of his people—that he will take from them their "heart of stone" and give them "a heart of flesh" [Ezek. 36:26]—openly testifies that what is of ourselves ought to be blotted out to convert us to righteousness; but that whatever takes its place is of him.
>
> (*Inst.* 2.3.8)

> *Nam quum bene volendi et agendi principium sit ex fide, videndum est unde sit ipsa fides. Quum vero gratuitum esse Dei donum clamet tota Scriptura, sequitur ex mera gratia esse ubi velle bonum incipimus, qui ad malum toto animo sumus naturaliter propensi. Ergo Dominus, ubi in populi sui conversione duo haec ponit, ut cor illi lapideum auferat, det carneum, aperte testatur oportere aboleri quod ex nobis est, quo ad iustitiam convertamur: quicquid autem in eius locum subit, a seipso esse.*
>
> (*OS* 3:282.25–33)

This passage is a rather complex tapestry, so for the rest of this section, I am going to tug at the threads in order to identify the key issues at stake. The crucial ones are corruption, sin and grace, faith as a gift, the will, conversion, and the completely new beginning brought about by grace.

Corruption and Grace

Let me begin with one of my favorites of Calvin's doctrines—our utter corruption and depravity. In this passage it appears in one phrase: "who are by nature inclined to evil with our whole heart." Not merely a part of us, such as our gut instincts that occasionally get the better of us, but in our whole being (*toto animo*) are we given over to evil (*ad malum*). And the reason: sin, especially original sin, which sets us on what may be called a "depraved default." Those with even a grain of knowledge about Calvin will immediately identify this as a resounding theme of his thought. And he certainly doesn't miss an opportunity to hammer the message home: in contrast to the noble and beautiful state of human beings (and nature) before the fall (Calvin 1847a, 137), we are in a quite bad state, full of evil, corruption, vice, and sin (*Inst.* 1.4.1–4; 1.5.11–15 and especially 2.1–5; *OS* 3:40–44, 55–60, 228–320). On this matter the writer in him often breaks forth:

> What then? Do you count yourself exempt from the number of those whose "feet are swift to shed blood" [Rom. 3:15], whose hands are fouled with robberies and murders, "whose throats are like open graves, whose tongues deceive, whose lips are envenomed" [Rom. 3:13]; whose works are useless, wicked, rotten, deadly; whose hearts are without God; whose inmost parts, depravities; whose eyes are set upon strategems; whose minds are eager to revile—to sum up, whose every part stands ready to commit infinite wickedness [Rom. 3:10-18]?
>
> (*Inst.* 2.3.3; *OS* 3:275.2–9)

We certainly had it drummed into us as children. Every one of my father's prayers included a request for the forgiveness of sins and a rescue from our inherently evil ways—whether it was before dinner or after the Bible reading after dinner, in a park before a picnic, at a wedding or a funeral, or in a child's prayer before going to sleep. At some level, I suspect it gave my father a perverse pleasure to tell people that they were hopeless sinners and worth nothing on their own. More than one parishioner found it annoying and depressing, and it left us as children with a deep feeling that we were worthless. Yet at one level my father was dead right, at least as far as Calvin was concerned.

But what has this got to do with grace, let alone radical grace? To begin with, it is a deeply democratic and egalitarian doctrine. Original sin, especially in its hereditary form (there is also imitation), is not a particularly popular doctrine these days (see *Inst.* 2.1.6–8; *OS* 3:234–38), but it does have a distinct democratic element to it that should not be discarded too quickly with the proverbial bathwater. It is, if you like, a *democracy of depravity*. The whole human race, Calvin writes, is involved "in the same guilt" (*Inst.* 1.6.1; *OS* 3:60.13–14). Not only everyone, but also every part of our existence is corrupt: "We are so vitiated and perverted in every part of our nature that by this great corruption we stand justly condemned and convicted by God. . . . For our nature is not only destitute and empty of good, but so fertile and fruitful of every evil that it cannot be idle" (*Inst.* 2.1.8; *OS* 3:237.8–10 and 238.7–9). No one can claim a superior status because of some achievement or because of inherited wealth, privilege, or power. The snobbish noble is exactly the same before God as the diseased peasant or prostitute. Or in our day, the drug-taking child molester is no different before God than the respected barrister or the power-suited businesswoman. To be sure, it is a democracy of the lowest common denominator: we're all scum; it's just that some hide it better than others. Too often the political punch of such a point is lost when the phrase "before God" is deployed. It refers merely to spiritual matters, some will say, and not to our status in society and politics. After all, they go on, there is a natural hierarchy of society, where some are blessed more than others with wealth, opportunity, and power—wealthy men from powerful families first, poor men second, women third. . . . My reply: we simply cannot quarantine Calvin's theological position from the realm of politics.

Further, the push to radical corruption has an inverse effect on grace. The more you emphasize how depraved and scumlike we really are, the more you grant to the power of grace. Calvin begins the *Institutes* in a similar fashion, stressing how the sinful and depressing nature of our existence shows us how great God is, and vice versa (see *Inst.* 1.1.1–3; *OS* 3:31–34). So also with grace: the harder you pull on the lever of sin, the higher grace goes. Here is Calvin from the passage I quoted at the beginning of this chapter: "When we, who are by nature inclined to evil with our whole heart, begin to will good, we do so out of mere grace [*ex mera gratia*]." Now grace starts to look like a radical doctrine, for radical corruption produces an even more radical grace. At this point the context of the passage I have quoted becomes important. The text comes in the midst of Calvin's discussion of some key biblical texts relating to our thoroughly corrupt and depraved nature. More specifically, he is in the process of answering the objection that divine grace and human will need to work together, for grace cannot do anything on its own (he draws on Jer. 32:39–40 and Ezek. 11:19; see also Calvin 1854a, 208–19; 1849a, 372–82). Calvin's response is unequivocal: there is no deal here, no tag-team effort, for the human will is utterly corrupt, and grace does the job entirely on its own. As if God would need a hand to save anyone!

Faith and Will

So grace, in response to absolute corruption, has become radically powerful. Or to put it in slightly different terms, grace is thoroughly undeserved and unearned. What then of faith? It is a simple objection that has been rehearsed thousands of times: is not faith a human attribute that opens us up to God? The answer is equally simple: faith is a gift of God. Or as Calvin puts it, "The whole of Scripture proclaims that faith is a free gift [*gratuitum . . . donum*] of God." Now, all of this is really Reformed Theology 101 (see *Inst.* 3.2; *OS* 4:6–54), but note what is happening: grace has climbed another point or two on the radical scale. So we have the following: in order to remain consistent with the radical doctrine of sin and depravity, Calvin must argue first that everything relies on grace since human beings can't do a thing for their own salvation. And that includes faith. Neither an active faith that seeks out God nor a passive faith that opens out to grace is the work of human beings. In fact, we don't have it in ourselves. So the perfectly logical step is to argue that the faith necessary for salvation comes from God, too (Calvin's thought really is rigorously consistent here). In the process, grace has become even more radical.

But there is more, for the human will, too, can do no good on its own. Once again the force of sin and depravity makes itself felt. Since Adam's freely willed sin, our will has lost its freedom and has been riveted onto sin (see *Inst.* 2.2; *OS* 3:241–71). So there is no possibility for the will (which is no longer free) to assist grace in any way whatsoever. But what if someone starts to show signs of a will that bends towards the good? The only possible conclusion is that God must have intervened. If someone begins "to will good," it can only be due to "mere grace."

So faith, the possibility of salvation, and good will are all due to grace. The reason: sin and depravity are so unimaginably foul. We can produce a simple formula: the more depraved we are, the more astonishing grace is. It is a direct ratio: anything you add to depravity, you must also add to grace. Or, as Calvin puts it, "Since the Lord, in bringing assistance, supplies us with what is lacking, the nature of that assistance will immediately make manifest its converse—viz. our penury" (*Inst.* 2.3.6; *OS* 2:279.5–7). It really is a case of putting all the eggs of salvation in one basket:

> We see how, not simply content to have given God due praise for our salvation, he [the psalmist] expressly excludes us from all participation in it. It is as if he were saying that not a whit remains to man to glory in, *for the whole is of God [quia totum a Deus est]*.
> (*Inst.* 2.3.6; *OS* 2:280.36–9; translation modified and emphasis added)

So far so good: grace has achieved a well-nigh stellar status, and we are in no doubt as to our somewhat parlous state. If this were a political analysis, then we would hear to no end how bad living conditions are and how life is a struggle. I do not mean that extra tax on luxury cars that came with the last national budget, or the fact that those on more than $150,000 per annum will no longer get the baby bonus, or the curfew of 1:00 a.m. for pubs, nightclubs, and other watering holes. It would be (to cull one example from any number) more like living in Baghdad than, say, Sydney; more like Darfur than New Zealand. Given that things have become so bad (and given that you don't have an oil-addicted greedy superpower looking for any excuse), the only viable solution would be nothing less than a revolution. And by revolution I mean a complete turnaround, an overthrow of all that was accepted as normal, a thorough change in the very coordinates by which our world is organized, a completely new start in which the old way of doing things has been swept away and an entirely new beginning has been made.

Conversion/Revolution

Sound familiar? It should, for it is the political version of conversion:

> Therefore, the Lord when he lays down these two principles in the conversion [*conversione*] of his people—that he will take from them their "heart of stone" and give them "a heart of flesh" [Ezek. 36:26]—openly testifies that what is of ourselves ought to be blotted out [*aboleri*] to convert [*convertamur*] us to righteousness; but that whatever takes its place is of him.
> (*Inst.* 2.3.8; *OS* 3:282.29–33)[1]

The gist of this passage is quite clear, for salvation entails a completely new beginning. And that beginning is entirely due to God's grace. Yet a few of the terms could do with some closer attention. The first is the use of the noun "conversion" (*conversio*) and then the verb "to convert" (*converto*). Both are compound words, based on the root *vert*, to turn, and the prefix *com* or *cum*. When they are put together, we get the

---

1. See also: "Hence it appears that God's grace, as this word is understood in discussing regeneration, is the rule of the Spirit to direct and regulate man's will. The Spirit cannot regulate without correcting, without reforming, without renewing. For this reason we say that the beginning of our regeneration is to wipe out what is ours" (*Inst.* 2.5.15; *OS* 3:315.7–13).

senses of turning around and reversing. Many of the early uses of the verb are of a military nature, referring to battle tactics of turning back the enemy, turning about the wing, or retreating in order to attack again. But then its more figurative meaning is to change or alter, to subvert and, especially for the noun, to *make a revolution*. Etymologically, then, the word that has come to have a purely spiritual sense—conversion—also has a political undercurrent. What Calvin means here is that one should undergo a thorough revolution, and that the source of that revolution is none other than God.

I have been slightly provocative here, but there are two further points from the passage that reinforce my argument. The first of these turns on that interesting verb *aboleri*, the passive infinitive of *aboleo*. It means to destroy or annihilate. Of course, the English derivative is "abolish," which captures the sense rather well. But what is to be annihilated? Nothing less than "what is of ourselves" (*quod ex nobis est*). That is a rather weak translation, for the Latin designates what makes us tick, our innermost being, who we are as human beings. *That* must be abolished and annihilated. As for what will be put in its place, it "is of himself" (*Inst.* 2.3.8). Once again the Latin is telling: "*a seipso esse*" (*OS* 3:282.33) means from within God's very own being. So the picture we have is an annihilation of what makes us who we are, and in its place God puts something that comes from deep inside his own being. The old order is obliterated, completely wiped out so that we can make a radically new beginning. The work of grace, it seems, is radically revolutionary, for it creates nothing less than new human beings.

Heart of Flesh

The skeptic will of course accuse me of ventriloquizing, of making Calvin speak with my own voice. So let me pick up one of Calvin's favored images—the heart of stone replaced by one of flesh. This is what "conversion" means, what is designated by the abolition of our old selves and the replacement by what comes from deep within God, but now with the concrete biblical images that Calvin loved so much. The image comes from Ezekiel 36:26–27, which Calvin cites a few lines earlier:

> "A new heart shall I give you, and will put a new spirit within you; and I will remove the heart of stone from your flesh, and give you a heart of flesh. And I shall put my Spirit within you, and cause

you to walk in my statutes" (Ezek. 36:26–27). Who shall say that the infirmity of the human will is strengthened by his help in order that it may aspire effectively to the choice of good, when it must rather be wholly transformed and renewed [*transformari renovarique totam*]? If in a stone there is such plasticity that, made softer by some means, it becomes somewhat bent, I will not deny that man's heart can be molded to obey the right, provided what is imperfect in him be supplied by God's grace. . . . If, therefore, a stone is transformed [*transformatur*] into flesh when God converts [*convertit*] us to zeal for the right, whatever is of our own will is effaced [*aboletur*]. What takes its place is wholly from God [*totum a Deo est*].

(*Inst.* 2.3.6; *OS* 3:279.18–280.3)

The context in Calvin's text is obviously the treatment of the will, especially the question of whether it can do anything to assist grace. In its own context, this text from Ezekiel is hardly about that theological conundrum. There it is concerned with what is needed for a return from exile in Babylon and the restoration of Judah. But the text serves admirably well in the way Calvin uses it.

But what jumps out from this passage are the hearts of stone and flesh. Conjuring up all manner of Bronze Age cardiac surgery procedures—what would they use to stitch the new heart in place? How would they keep the patient alive during surgery? What about rejection?—it is as graphic as it is effective. Yet the point is equally as obvious: this is a qualitative change from an unfeeling, stubborn, and indeed poorly functioning heart to one of flesh, one that pulses and beats, one that has feelings of remorse and longing and love.[2]

Before we go any further, I must confess that I am guilty of a slippage in the previous paragraph. In English the figurative "heart" is a symbol of feelings, of love and hate, of remorse and joy. This sense doubles over with the sense that the "heart" is also our inner emotive core. Actually, we seem to operate with a triple hierarchy: the head is the cool, calm zone of reason and reflection; the heart is our often-troubled emotional center; and our gut is the place for animal instincts like lust, gluttony, and other "gut instincts." Now, "heart" in Calvin's Latin has a different register: *cor* is much closer to what we would think of as the head. *Cor* is the mind as well as the soul of a person—from where our "core"

---

2. Calvin has a wonderful comment on the comparable Ezek. 11: 9–20: "A stone by its own hardness repels even the strongest blows of the hammers, and nothing can be inscribed on it; but the fleshy heart by its softness admits whatever is inscribed or engraven upon it" (Calvin 1849a, 373–74). It is an appropriate metaphor, he says, for a "rude and gross people."

derives. Indeed, it often stands in for "person" itself. It can also refer to the emotions, but they are secondary and closer to the gut. So when Calvin refers to the "*cor novum*" (new heart), the "*cor lapideum*" (heart of stone), and the "*cor carneum*" (heart of flesh), the sense conveyed is a little different from what we would associate with "heart." It is still the center of one's being, our "soul," as some might put it, but what constitutes that "core" is a little different. One last linguistic point: Calvin knew the occasional Hebrew word, so he may well have known that the word *lēv* (usually translated as "heart") actually means both mind and heart, reason and feelings, the seat of calm reflection and powerful emotions. This comprehensive Hebrew sense actually strengthens Calvin's point, especially since he knew at least some Hebrew: it is a thorough and qualitative change that includes everything. So we can expand the image: the divine heart transplant surgery actually involves the mind as well. In fact, we may as well speak of a "person transplant." The person of stone—hardheaded, unfeeling, and stubborn—is replaced with a real person who can think, reason, feel, and love.

Too often Calvin is attributed with the idea that human beings are "by nature" corrupt and default to sin when given half a chance. That assumption comes to grief with the passage I have been discussing. Not only does human nature change with the fall (*Inst.* 1.15; 2.1–5; *OS* 3:173–87, 228–320), passing from nobility to corruption, but it also undergoes a radical transformation with redemption. There is no unchangeable and essential human nature here.

My conclusion by now should be obvious: Calvin's argument pushes us to no other option than that God performs a revolutionary act of grace. The key lies in the verbs Calvin uses in the passage I quoted above: *transformari* and *transformatur* from *transformo*, to change in shape or transform; *renovari* from *renovo*, to refresh or re-create; and *convertit* (*converto*), which we have previously discussed with its sense of turning around, conversion, and revolution. And just to hammer the point home, Calvin concludes the passage we have been discussing with "whatever is of our own will is effaced [*aboletur*]. What takes its place is wholly from God [*totum a Deo est*]."

I don't think I am out of place at all to call this Calvin's revolution. Simply put, since the situation here is so bad, since we are so depraved and perverted through sin, it requires a complete abolition of the old and a thorough re-creation. This is the task of grace, to perform nothing less than divine surgery, remove the heart of stone, and put in its place the heart of flesh. But note something unique about this revolutionary theology: all the revolutions we know have in some way or another assumed that the initiative begins with human beings. It may be the quiet revolution of Quebec in the 1960s, the October Revolution in Russia in 1917, the bourgeois revolutions that first began in France over 1789–1799, the revolution that ended apartheid in South Africa during 1990–1994, or even the American Revolution of 1775–1783, and many more. But all of them share the same feature: human beings are responsible. Those of the old order are responsible for its corruption and decay, and the revolutionaries are responsible for the new order that promises so much (although rarely delivers). Calvin's theological revolution agrees on the first point: human beings are indeed responsible for the woeful state of things. But he differs sharply on the second: we human beings simply cannot carry out a successful revolution. Only God can do that.

ROPING GRACE BACK IN

So Calvin is in a situation where he has a radical doctrine of revolutionary grace on his hands. Due to human sin and corruption, we are facing a complete conversion/transformation/re-creation/revolution in God's hands. But what does he do next? Instead of letting grace have its head, he ropes it back in. Choose your image: reining in a spirited horse, roping a bucking steer, hauling back an eager dog, or carefully channeling a torrent of tumbling, racing water. Or add one of your own. They all capture what I see happening with the doctrine of grace in Calvin's work.

Calvin explores a couple of paths in order to bring grace under control: (1) a careful itinerary for grace, designating what it cannot do, what it can do, and when it can do so; and (2) the doctrine of predestination, or what I like to call the aristocracy of salvation. I begin with the careful effort to control and order grace.

Neatly Ordered Grace

As before, I begin with a key text or two and look at them closely. There are two, one from the *Institutes* and one, tellingly, from his commentary on Romans:

> Let us sum these up. Christ was given to us by God's generosity, to be grasped and possessed by us in faith. By partaking of him, we principally receive a double grace: namely, that being reconciled to God through Christ's blamelessness, we may have in heaven instead of a Judge a gracious Father; and secondly, that sanctified by his spirit we may cultivate blamelessness and purity of life.
> (*Inst.* 3.11.1; translation modified)

> *Summa autem haec fuit, Christum nobis Dei benignitate datum, fide a nobis apprehendi ac possideri, cuius participatione duplicem potissimum gratiam recipiamus: nempe ut eius innocentia Deo reconciliati, pro iudice iam propitium habeamus in caelis Patrem: deinde ut eius Spiritu sanctificati, innocentiam puritatemque vitae meditemur.*
> (*OS* 4:182.3–8)

While the immediate context for this quotation is the opening of a long discussion of justification by faith, the sine qua non is nothing less than grace. Should we have any doubts, then the following slice from the commentary on Romans 6:14—"not under law, but under grace"—should put those to rest.

> Under the name of grace, we understand likewise both parts of redemption, that is, the remission of sins, whereby God imputeth righteousness unto us; and the sanctification of the Spirit, by the which he frameth us anew unto good works.
> (Calvin 1844b, 159)[3]

Both texts talk about two carefully defined stages: reconciliation and then sanctification. And just to tie up any loose ends, the first involves Christ and the second brings in the Holy Spirit, all the while pivoting on the Father. When I read these texts, the image that comes to mind is that of a wild river carefully channeled by means of levees and sandbags. At first it rushes through chasms and tumbles over rocks, the terrain of wild-water canoeists, but then soon afterwards the river is harnessed, directed by walls and channels, dammed and tamed. That is precisely what Calvin does to grace in these texts.

---

3. I use here the translation published in 1844 by the Calvin Translation Society, partly to acknowledge a curious coincidence. As I began to come to terms with Calvin, I spied a full collection of his commentaries available secondhand and rather cheaply. I gave in, bought them, only to find that they came from the library of a longtime mentor and friend, David Gunn. Of course, my father asks me regularly how my collection of Calvin's commentaries is faring. "Do you use them?" he asks. "Whenever I check Calvin's exegesis in preparing for a sermon, I first think, 'Is that all!' But then I realize how profound it is."

Now for some exegesis: the text from the *Institutes* begins with the word "*summa.*" This is more than a mere "summary" or "summing up," as the translations put it. *Summa* actually means the top or summit, so here it refers to the essence of the matter, its chief point. The word also came to refer to one's major work, if one happened to be a writer or theologian—the most well known is certainly Thomas Aquinas's *Summa theologica* (although Calvin was not so enamored of this father of the Schoolmen). So this is the *summa*, the defining statement, but of what? Of nothing less than salvation. In the preceding sentence, Calvin writes, "I believe I have already explained above, with sufficient care, how for men cursed under the law there remains, in faith, one sole means of recovering salvation. I believe I have also explained what faith itself is, and those benefits of God which it confers upon man, and the fruits it brings forth" (*Inst.* 3.11.1; *OS* 4:181.35–182.2). So what Calvin is doing here is nothing less than stating as succinctly as possible (sometimes a little difficult for him) the defining statement of salvation.

And that statement (the first text quoted above) begins with the idea that Christ is given (*datum*) to us, and we grasp and possess him by faith (*fide*). Even here it is very neatly organized. There are two preliminary steps, one of giving by God and the other of grasping. Each of these has two further steps, for the gift of God is both Christ and faith, and our act of apprehending by faith involves both seizing (the gerund *apprehendi*) and taking possession (*possideri*).

This is extraordinarily neat. Two by two we march on, like the animals in the story of Noah and the flood, or like a major I once knew from the Black Watch Regiment based in Montreal. He would place all his socks and underwear in neat, careful piles within the draw. His shoes were carefully arranged and always highly polished. Calvin and this major would have gotten on famously. As would my father: he gained fame for the idea that everything should have its place—a bolt from 1973 (next to the one from 1972), the pair of pliers (next to the shifting spanners), Winston Churchill's brilliant piece of propaganda called *The History of World War Two* (next to *Stalin's Wars*). And everything fit into its allotted place, with no room to spare. Neat, tidy, and apparently well-organized—I write "apparently" because he was actually badly organized. Not only did he put an immense amount of effort into keeping things arranged in this way, but it always took an eternity for him to get something out. None of this putting your hand on what you need in an instant. I suspect that the careful arrangement of books and photos and tools was a desperate effort to gain control of the many other disorganized parts of his life. (I'm afraid I am much the same these days.)

We are not done with the march of the twos, for Calvin himself identifies the two steps or the "the double grace" that accrues from the previous gifts of Christ and faith: reconciliation and sanctification. The Latin here reads "*duplicem . . . gratiam.*" Grace in two steps! Is that not the most significant sign of ordering and directing grace? Grace Part A can go in this file, and Grace Part B in that one.

By now we should expect some more neat arrangements, and Calvin does not disappoint. In the first, reconciliation through the righteousness or blamelessness of Christ, we find that God switches sides, moving from a judge on one side to an indulgent or well-disposed Father (*propitium . . . Patrem*) on the other. And if we look closer, we find that reconciliation itself has two steps. At this point I would like to bring in the text from the Romans commentary, where we also find that grace is carefully organized. Here Calvin phrases the first stage a little differently: it is a matter of the remission of sins. But that cannot happen without the imputation of righteousness to us by God (see also *Inst.* 2.17; *OS* 3:508–15). In other words, our sins will not be forgiven without being cloaked in God's righteousness—something that Christ manages to do for us so that we can stand before God as though we were righteous and thereby get him to make the costume switch from stern judge to loving Father.

All of which is merely the first step in the "twofold grace." The second is none other than sanctification through the Spirit, as both our texts make abundantly clear. Christ may carry out the first step, but now the Holy Spirit comes in on a tag-team play and completes the second. But what is "to be sanctified [*sanctificati*]?" A combination of *sanctus*, holy or consecrated, and *ficeo*, make—so, to make holy—sanctification involved for Calvin another two steps. One must aspire to blamelessness and purity (*innocentiam puritatemque*). But note here that it also involves being Christlike, for he too has *innocentia*, which may also mean uprightness or righteousness.

I realize that I am laboring the point a little, but it does show through with remarkable resilience: Calvin likes things neatly organized and ordered. And he likes nothing more ordered than the powerful and revolutionary doctrine of grace. This continual desire on his part shows up in another feature of the texts I have been exegeting. We not only find a series of twos, but there is also a correct sequence: grace means the gift of Christ and the faith through which we apprehend that gift. It then leads onto the remission of our sins, which can happen only through Christ's blamelessness, which is transposed onto us through the cross and thereby reconciles us to God. Then it moves onto sanctification by the Spirit and its attendant purity and uprightness on our part.[4] Now, to be fair to Calvin, the very fact that we need to write in such narrative form, that the words and sentences must follow one another, produces a need to come up with a narrative sequence when writing about something like salvation. It is at heart a story. Yet in many cases the whole drama may also be seen as simultaneous: gift of Christ, death, faith, remission, reconciliation, and sanctification really can take place in one explosive event. But then Calvin loves arranging all these things when he can. I keep thinking of Noah. In the face of a massive catastrophe and spectacular saving event, Noah must first patiently build an ark, step by step and according to the instructions, and then the animals must come in two by two. No fluster here, just calm order.

From the Democracy of Depravity to the Aristocracy of Salvation

The more famous—or, depending on one's perspective, infamous—way in which Calvin restrains grace is through predestination. The doctrine itself is quite straightforward:

> We call predestination God's eternal decree, by which he compacted with himself what he willed to become of each man. For all are not created in equal condition; rather, eternal life is foreordained for some, eternal damnation for others. Therefore, as any man has been created to one or other of these ends, we speak of him as predestined to life or to death.
> (*Inst.* 3.21.5; *OS* 4:374.11–17; see also Calvin 1849b, 477–79)

It seems to me that predestination may well be described as the aristocracy of salvation, an aristocracy that stands in a curious imbalance with Calvin's democracy of depravity. My father's parishioners—usually the

---

4. The examples multiply. I can't note them all, but Calvin also has a liking for lists, as the following example shows all too well: "But the matter cannot be summed up in briefer form than in the eighth chapter of the book *On Rebuke and Grace to Valentinus*. There Augustine first teaches: the human will does not obtain grace by freedom, but obtains freedom by grace; when the feeling of delight has been imparted through the same grace, the human will is formed to endure; it is strengthened with unconquerable fortitude; controlled by grace, it never will perish, but, if grace forsake it, it will straightway fall; by the Lord's free mercy it is converted to good, and once converted it perseveres in good; the direction of the human will toward good, and after direction its continuation in good, depend solely on God's will, not upon any merit of man" (*Inst.* 2.3.14; *OS* 3:290.19–29).

well-heeled and powerful ruling elite of Australian country towns—were much more comfortable with being part of the saved aristocracy than with the depraved masses. The problem was that whenever my father was able, he delighted in reminding them that they were part of the latter.

The tension goes as follows. Everyone is equally sinful and equally condemned for it. As I argued earlier, the abolition of any salvation by works closes down any possible claim to merit or privilege. But then Calvin says, You may all be depraved, but that doesn't mean you will all be saved. In other words, grace is limited (see *Inst.* 2.3.10; *OS* 3:285.9–286.24). However, the problem runs deeper than this, for there is a fundamental contradiction in the very engine room of Calvin's theology. Since predestination is an eternal decree of God, it undermines the radically democratic effect of his doctrine of sin and thereby of the revolutionary potential of grace. I will come back to this contradiction in a moment.

In the meantime, a couple of other features jump out when you read key chapters (*Inst.* 3.21, but see also 3.22–24; *OS* 4:368–79 and 379–432) on predestination. Calvin is extremely defensive concerning predestination, admitting on more than one occasion that it is a difficult doctrine, with plenty of pitfalls. On this issue he does not follow his characteristic path of stating the main issue and then exploring it in relation to the Bible before dealing with objections. You get the distinct feeling that he has been savaged on this matter before: we find comments concerning the secret things of God and those matters that lurk in the recesses of divine wisdom; a caution not to speculate on a matter like predestination beyond what the Bible says but also to avoid shutting one's mouth completely;[5] and tirades against petulant scoffers, boiling critics, raging reviewers, and furious madmen (the terms are all his, but I plan to use them). Only then, after all of this huffing and puffing, does he actually offer a definition (the one I quoted above). In other words, Calvin gives one the distinct sense that he is rather anxious about this doctrine. And that nervousness is not merely because he had some opponents to deal with (there are plenty of those through the *Institutes*), nor is it because he fretted over the response of the faithful to this doctrine. It goes much further: the text betrays an awareness that predestination runs straight against his democratic take on human corruption and depravity. Above all, it clips the wings of radical grace.

---

5. At this point I can't resist at least this quotation: "Let us, I say, permit the Christian man to open his mind and ears to every utterance of God directed to him, provided it be with such restraint that when the Lord closes his holy lips, he also shall at once close the way to inquiry" (*Inst.* 3.21.3; 4:372.7–11).

There is a second signal of this tension in Calvin's thought: the word "grace" turns up with telltale frequency. Predestination is—Calvin tries to assure us—a manifestation of God's grace. In a comment repeated a billion times afterwards by those who take after Calvin, he points out that it is a mark of God's abounding grace that some are saved at all. This is about as radical as grace gets in the discussion of predestination. Indeed, in an effort to rivet grace onto predestination, he ends up calling it "his gratuitous election [*gratuita eius electio*]" (*Inst.* 3.21.7; *OS* 4:377.21). Or more extensively:

> As Scripture, then, clearly shows, we say that God once established by his eternal and unchangeable plan those whom he long before determined once for all to receive into salvation, and those whom, on the other hand, he would devote to destruction. *We assert that, with respect to the elect, this plan was founded upon his freely given mercy* [*gratuita*], without regard to human worth; but by his just and irreprehensible judgment he has barred the door of life to those whom he has given over to damnation.
> (*Inst.* 3.21.7; *OS* 4:378.31–379.3; emphasis added)

This quotation draws our discussion back to the fundamental tension between the democracy of depravity and the aristocracy of predestination. The clause I emphasized above brings it home: "We assert that, with respect to the elect, this plan was founded upon his freely given mercy [*gratuita*]." "Freely given mercy" is a long-winded way of translating "grace." In other words, grace pertains only to the elect and not to those doomed to destruction. If one holds to predestination, and if grace pertains to the process of salvation, then grace can operate only with the elect. A very restricted conversion/transformation/re-creation/revolution, is it not?

Despite all Calvin's impeccable logic on the question of predestination, there is a deeper problem that is far less logical. Let me put it this way: it is not as though everyone in the democratic mass of the depraved gathers at the gate of salvation only to find that some are admitted and the rest not. No, this democratic crowd is cut in two with a prior class distinction, for "all are not created in equal condition [*non enim pari conditione creatur omnes*]; rather, eternal life is foreordained for some, eternal damnation for others" (*Inst.* 3.21.5; *OS* 4:374.13–15). So Calvin has not quite abolished ranking in terms of privilege or inheritance. He may have removed any privilege or status according to the merit of works, but he has replaced it with the distinction between the elect and the damned. There is no better way to describe this than as an aristocracy of salvation.

THE REVOLUTIONARY PARADOX

There are two ways we can read this tension within Calvin between the revolution of grace and its careful ordering, between a democratic depravity and an aristocratic election. The first way is to take Ernst Troeltsch's (1992) well-worn distinction between charisma and institution, or sect and church. In this case we would argue that the great rush of the Reformation, with its discovery of justification by faith through grace, is the classic moment of charisma that breaks through the ossified status quo and stale practice of religious life. But then, while charisma is wonderful for inspiring new directions, for bringing about revolutionary fervor and inciting the passions, it is a poor basis for long-term success. Prophets and firebrands do not make the best organizers, largely because they can't sit in one spot for too long. In order to make the spirit last, we need the machine men, the dour administrators, finance people, and building inspectors. Charisma needs structure; the spirit needs a home in order to settle down. All too many movements have fired up the imagination, only to fade away once the flame has dimmed. Then everyone stands around blaming everyone else for running the cart into the mud. On this schema Calvin becomes the careful administrator, the ordered thinker who codifies the spirit in a structured and well-thought-out system.

The catch is that Calvin is a little more complex than this, for the tension is not between him as systematic organizer and the spiritual fire that preceded him. The tension lies within him and his thought. And since the tension between charisma and institution has become overly worn, I would prefer instead to speak of one between revolution and reaction. So in closing this chapter, I explore the tension between revolutionary outbreak and repression.

Here we face a basic problem of any movement for renewal: the outbreak of freedom all too often finds itself tied back down under new forms of repression. Such repression may take two forms: In one form, a protest for freedom may be crushed by the police, the protestors jailed, and the organization banned. In this case it succumbs to existing forms of repression, as anyone who has taken to the streets can attest. Apart from the police with their batons, shields, and water cannon, the drawn-out court cases suck all the energy from the protestors as they try to stay out of prison. Breaking radical individuals and groups through the labyrinth of the courts and the clogging mud of legal proceedings is a well-honed approach. On the other hand, the protest may turn into a mass movement: the old order is then thrown out, and a new start is made. Sadly, before too long the new leaders become dictators, repression follows, and freedom quickly flies out the window.

In this second form, the paradox of revolution shows up in all its ugly brutality. The examples are endless: Pol Pot in Cambodia, the Boer resistance to the British Empire and the ensuing apartheid regime, the American Revolution and the American Empire, the establishment of the State of Israel and the repression of the Palestinians, Mao Zedong and the Cultural Revolution, and on and on. The pattern has been repeated with sickening regularity through the last century or two. May I suggest, somewhat provocatively, that Calvin also embodies this tension in his texts? Grace may be a life-changing, indeed a world-changing, experience, but it runs all too quickly into a controlling and repressive regime. It may come as a response to our absolute depravity and inability to do a thing to save ourselves, but it can lead to a more rigorous imprisonment. It may utterly abolish our former life and give us a completely new one, but all too often the new one bears a striking resemblance to the old one.

In closing, let us return to our old friend, the cat in the bag. Perhaps the best way to picture this struggle over grace is in terms of this poor cat. There, at last, is the opening it has been waiting for. The rope is loosened, light pours in, and he makes a lightning-fast leap for freedom. But the exulting cry is cut off all too quickly. With reflexes faster than a cat, Calvin clamps his hand over the mouth of the bag. With the other, he pushes the cat back in and scrabbles around for the rope. Our revolutionary cat has been trapped.

4
Freedom
The Liberty of the Gospel

At this point I can imagine that some readers, especially Calvin advocates, may feel that I have engaged more in eisegesis (reading into) than exegesis (reading out of). Even though the wiser ones may see that any interpretation is a good mix of both, they may still feel that eisegesis dominates. The tension is more of my own making—the argument will go—and I have merely found Calvin to be a convenient sounding board for it. That sense will quickly disappear with the third great topic I consider: *libertas Christiana*, Christian freedom, or liberty.

Let me begin with a story: In the great epic poem *The Odyssey*, Homer famously describes the passage of Odysseus and his ship through a narrow strait. On either side are two monsters, one called Scylla and the other Charybdis. While the names are all too familiar, what they mean is not. Scylla is a real beauty, with six long necks equipped with grisly heads, each of which contains three rows of sharp teeth. Her body consists of twelve canine legs and a cat's tail. On the other side, Charybdis is a monstrous mouth who swallows huge amounts of water three times a day before belching it back out again, creating large whirlpools. An arrow's shot apart, the problem with Scylla and Charybdis is that if you try to avoid one, you are caught by the other.[1]

---

1. A fear of women lurks behind these mythological figures, with one the all-devouring and many-headed woman who will consume a man whole, and the other the huge, sucking whirlpool that draws a man in, never to reemerge.

In his passage through the strait, Odysseus acts on the advice of the nymph Circe and steers closer to Scylla, for Circe had warned him that Charybdis would sink his whole ship. Just as the ship passes the strait, Scylla swoops and devours six of his men. Odysseus takes up the empty space and rows the ship out of harm's way . . . or almost, for his men had offended Helios by killing the god's sacred cattle. Zeus retaliates by destroying ship and crew (except Odysseus) with a thunderbolt. Stranded on a makeshift raft, Odysseus is swept back through the strait to face Scylla and Charybdis again. This time he passes near Charybdis, and his raft is sucked into her vast mouth. Odysseus survives by clinging to a fig tree growing on the rock overhanging her lair—literally caught between a rock and a hard place. On the next outflow of water, Charybdis spits the raft out; Odysseus recovers it and paddles away.

I have told this story for more reasons than my love of the classics. The main reason is to give a little more background to the sense that Calvin is much like Odysseus (and to give some depth to the phrase "between Scylla and Charybdis"). In other words, Calvin is really trying to weave his own perilous path between the Scylla of unbridled and anarchistic freedom and the Charybdis of having Christian freedom sucked back into legalism.

His goal is quite clear. Christian liberty is absolutely necessary: "Unless this freedom be comprehended [*nisi ea tenetur*], neither Christ nor gospel truth, nor inner peace of soul, can be rightly known [*recte cognoscitur*]" (*Inst.* 3.19.1; *OS* 4:282.34–283.1). His *teneo* may well have a stronger sense in this case, such as "grasp" or "master." It is crucial to grasp Christian freedom, Calvin says, since the gospel is simply incomplete without it. In fact, freedom follows hard on the heels of justification (*Inst.* 3.19.1), and for that reason it is an absolutely necessary if somewhat tricky subject.

In order to get to this goal, Calvin has some hard rowing ahead. His overriding strategy is to avoid the snapping heads of Scylla's radical freedom. But why does Calvin work so hard to distance himself from anarchistic radicalism? It was nothing less than the fright he gained from the *Affaire des Placards* of 1534, the Peasants' War of 1525, and the Kingdom of Münster of 1534–1535 (see my discussion in chapter 1).

In response to these events and their "misreadings" of the Bible, Calvin follows two main strategies. The first is a sustained effort to specify precisely what "Christian freedom" really means. A little like his effort with grace, this resembles an attempt to channel a wild brook into a quiet stream. It turns out that there are different types of liberty:

the freedom from the law that comes from looking only to Christ; the inner freedom to obey the will of God (once one is freed from the law); and the full liberty in external matters relating to one's practice of the faith. The second strategy involves the construction and then deployment of a crucial distinction—private versus public, or spiritual versus temporal. In all of this Calvin tries to block the interpretations of the radicals while desperately avoiding the sucking whirlpool of legalism.

CURTAILING FREEDOM

Calvin sets out to limit freedom in what is for him a well-tried fashion: he specifies what types of freedom he will allow, or rather, what he feels the Bible will allow. Here we find a characteristic effort to box and organize a central Christian doctrine. The problem is that Calvin struggles to do so: he sets out to provide careful parameters to freedom only to risk things getting out of hand. He sets those parameters by specifying three types of Christian liberty. Here he describes the first type:

> Christian freedom, in my opinion, consists of three parts. The first: that the consciences of believers, in seeking assurance of their justification before God, should rise above and advance beyond the law, forgetting all law righteousness. . . . Removing, then, mention of law, and laying aside all consideration of works, we should, when justification is being discussed, embrace God's mercy [*Dei misericordiam*] alone, turn our attention from ourselves, and look only to Christ.
> (*Inst.* 3.19.2; *OS* 4:283.3–7, 13–17)

For Calvin, Christian freedom is nothing less than an issue of the law versus grace, or of justification by works or by faith. In other words, it goes right to the heart of the gospel. But freedom means quite specifically freedom *from* the law and freedom *for* Christ. And to carry on the prepositional connections, it is freedom *through* grace and *by* faith. In other words, it is not merely freedom on its own, freedom as a free-floating value of itself. Yet this seemingly innocuous statement—freedom is freedom from the law and for Christ, by faith and through grace—is pure gunpowder. We may have dampened it through our familiarity and repetitions, not keeping our powder as dry as we should, but let us try to recover its freshness. Imagine saying to someone, You are free from the law because Christ died for you! A dangerous doctrine, is it not?

The second type of Christian freedom follows:

> The second part, dependent upon the first, is that consciences observe the law, not as if constrained by the necessity of the law, but that freed from the law's yoke they willingly obey God's will.
> (*Inst.* 3.19.4; *OS* 4:284.28–30)

Sometimes Calvin seems like an old fogy, a real fossil of five centuries ago,[2] but at other times he seems astonishingly modern. This text is one of those latter moments. The key to obeying the law, he writes, is inner compulsion, a deep inner need that arises from one's genuine core, the center of one's being. How true, we might want to say. Let me give two examples.

In Denmark (a place I know rather well) the Danish (Lutheran) Church is still the established state church. This means that priests are paid by the state, the churches are maintained through taxes, there is a government minister for the churches, and the royal family is by default part of the church. In contrast, I come from a country where we have no one established church, and where all churches have to support themselves, their clergy, and their property. In a recent discussion with a priest (her name is Pernille) in the Danish church, I began pointing out the advantages of the Danish situation: the church has a greater role in society as a whole, confirmation is a rite of passage for many teenagers, theology is a respectable career and not a pseudoscience (as many in Australia think), and people are used to the clergy performing important rituals on major social and national occasions. But for Pernille all of this was the sign of a problem. This external observance, she pointed out to me, is the death of the church. She was one of those who wanted the church to be disestablished, as in Sweden, for only then would genuine commitment from the heart show itself. Only then would the church really need to work to survive. It is exactly the same point that Calvin makes.

Another example is England, where a series of archaic church laws date back to the end of the seventeenth century. In 1699 the Apostasy Act came into force: it stipulated that anyone who should choose to leave the Church of England would be stripped of civil rights, fined,

---

2. One such moment comes in the following comment on sleep: "Indeed, sleep itself, which benumbs man, seeming even to deprive him of life, is no obscure witness of immortality, since it suggests not only thoughts of things that have never happened, but also presentiments of the future" (*Inst.* 1.15.2; *OS* 3:175.34–37). Or perhaps this is the source of a possible New Age Calvin. . . .

and thrown in prison. It was surely designed to stop the appeal of the Roman Catholics and the various Dissenting churches, such as the Baptists, Presbyterians, or Congregationalists. On top of this, there was the Blasphemy Act, which carried with it a hefty fine and a year in prison—mainly designed to put an end to political attacks on the venal and self-serving parsons and the church itself from that long tradition of British radicalism. But my favorite would have to be the Sunday Observance Act: if someone could not give a good excuse for missing church, then he or she may well be ushered into a prison cell for up to six weeks and fined. Apparently there were zealous justices of the peace who still tried to enforce this law in some rural areas in the middle of the nineteenth century. Once again the question is, How can this elaborate collection of external compulsions make anyone believe? Here it is a prime case of being "constrained by the necessity of the law" and being under the "law's yoke," as Calvin puts it. Needless to say, it also let the clergy in the Church of England off the hook from any genuine work with their parishes. No wonder the English parson became for so long a byword for self-interest, favoritism, corruption, and lack of concern for parishioners.

Yet the reason that this focus on inner compulsion seems so modern to us is that it is part of that newish invention known as the private individual subject. As I will argue a little later, Calvin had a good hand in the invention of this new creature. He stands near its source and gives it a very good shove along. A crucial feature of that individual is the truth of the inner self and the falsity of what is on the outside. Do we not still refer to the mask we put on for external observers as a mask that conceals our real selves?

The legacy of this category of Christian freedom is as radical as the first category, except that now it tends towards the ideology and practice of liberalism. Does that mean that Calvin is a liberal ideologue too? Yes indeed, at least on this point (see Tawney 1926, 112). For those of us who find liberalism stale and hypocritical, I suggest that we forget too readily how unsettling and revolutionary liberalism was in its early days. Calvin could hardly foresee where this private individualism, which leads one to base his or her actions on inner compulsion, might lead, but it would become a centerpiece for the bourgeois revolutions of the eighteenth and nineteenth centuries; the push for representative democracies, in which each person had the right to vote privately and without compulsion; the declarations of the "Rights of Man"; the major victories of feminism and the rights of children; and so on (see du Cros 1999; Stevenson 1999, 21–32; Chappuis 1987).[3] Calvin is a contributor—or in Weberian terms a "vanishing mediator"—to this stream, although in ways that he could hardly see. He may have felt that a focus on the inner desire to obey God conveniently quarantined his second point from any political implications, but it was not to be.

Finally, there is the third effort to contain freedom:

> The third part of Christian freedom lies in this: regarding outward things that are of themselves indifferent [ἀδιάφορα], we are not bound before God by any religious obligation preventing us from sometimes using them and other times not using them, indifferently. And the knowledge of this freedom is very necessary for us, for if it is lacking, our consciences will have no repose and there will be no end to superstitions [*superstitionum*].
> (*Inst.* 3.19.7; *OS* 4:286.27–32)

This one is perhaps the most interesting of the lot. Initially it seems like a strange subject, as Calvin points out. Why, he asks, raise the matter of what you eat, or what you wear, or what you do on public holidays with their dubious activities? But then he does two things. The first is to take the hard line: everything is lawful for the one who truly believes. This is how he reads Paul's statement in Romans 14:14: "Nothing is unclean in itself; but it is unclean for anyone who thinks it is unclean."[4] In other words, if you think something is unclean, if you begin worrying about it, then you still need to get to the point of realizing that it is your own problem and not the thing in question. Calvin has a wonderful passage (one of those where he lets his literary flair take off) where he traces the way someone who begins doubting the use of linen for sheets, shirts, napkins, and handkerchiefs will end up doubting hemp or even the use of napkins themselves. Or with a fine wine, doubts lead one to drink a rough one and then to drink only pure water. Or, closer to our own time, concern about the content of a book or a movie—for example, the incredibly popular Harry Potter series—will all too soon lead one to stop reading or watching movies altogether since they are all suspect in some way. Take one step, and the slide down the proverbial slope begins. So Calvin states it quite clearly: "We should use God's

---

3. For an excellent reassessment of Calvin's own attitudes towards women, freedom, and the church, see Douglass (1985).
4. See also his comments on external ceremonies, which "have now been abolished by the coming of Christ," in his commentary on Galatians (Calvin 1854b, 19).

gifts for the purpose for which he gave them to us, with no scruple of conscience, no trouble of mind. With such confidence our minds will be at peace with him, and will recognize his liberality toward us" (*Inst.* 3.19.8; *OS* 4:288.7–11). Rest at ease, he says, and be sure that in God's eyes all things are pure and simply use them for his glory. After all, they are merely external and therefore unremarkable and indifferent (the sense of the Greek ἀδιάφορα). In other words, they are neutral and therefore should not bother us.

Now, this is a rather radical position. The usual reading is to point out that it is fine to have a clear and free conscience about these matters, but that we might want to be careful about our weaker brethren. Complete freedom in external matters is fine, goes the argument, but we need to watch out for those weaker in the faith and more sensitive than we are (note how the weaker comrade is always someone else). Calvin does in fact go on to discuss the key biblical texts on this matter in the later parts of the section on Christian liberty (see especially the discussion of Rom. 14:1, 13; 15:1; 1 Cor. 8:9; 10:25, 29, 32; Gal. 5:13 in *Inst.* 3.19.11; *OS* 4:290.9–291.13). And he does introduce the distinction between offense given to the weak and offense taken by the malevolent; in the case of the first, one must be careful, while the second lot should be ignored and told to get lost. As he sets out in characteristic fashion to find a moderate position between two extremes (avoid offending the weak and giving an excuse to the malevolent keen to pick up on a slip), Calvin seems to be softening his hard line (*Inst.* 3.19.8–13; *OS* 4:287–93). But just when we think he has become a softie, he recovers his radical position: "Now, since believers' consciences, having received the privilege of their freedom, which we previously described, have, by Christ's gift, attained to this, that they should not be entangled with any snares of observances in those matters in which the Lord has willed them to be free, we conclude that *they are released from the power of all men*" (*Inst.* 3.19.14; *OS* 4:293.16–20; emphasis mine). Back on message, Calvin really does push the hard line. Christian freedom really means complete freedom from the observance of external things, indeed from human authority concerning those things.

On three counts Calvin has tried to steer clear of Scylla's heads only to find that he draws ever closer to her. Had he been Odysseus, by this time Scylla would have snapped up six of his sailors. Despite his best efforts to curtail freedom, it seems to get more and more out of hand: first, freedom from the law through justification in Christ is a deeply radical proposition; second, freedom from outer compulsion and of the inner desire to obey God marks a fundamental shift to the value of inner freedom; third, freedom from concern over external things renders outer observance null and void. We seem to have a genuinely radical view of freedom.

PRIVATE AND PUBLIC

I imagine Calvin standing back from his writing desk, pondering what he has just written. Have I nailed it and dealt with Christian freedom adequately? Have I forestalled those damned placard wielders, radical Anabaptists, and Müntzerites? Is popish legalism put well away? But just when he begins to relax, he jumps and realizes that he has left the door wide open for those radicals and anarchists. Freedom from the law, the liberty of one's inner compulsion, and freedom from concern over external observance—all these could easily be read in a political direction! Christian freedom is just a little too free for comfort. We need something else, and that is nothing other than a new distinction.

So he picks up his quill and resumes writing:

> For, as soon as Christian freedom is mentioned, either passions boil or wild tumults rise unless these wanton spirits are opposed in time, who otherwise most wickedly corrupt the best things. Some, on the pretext of this freedom, shake off all obedience toward God and break out into unbridled license. Others disdain it, thinking that it takes away all moderation, order, and choice of things. What should we do here, hedged about with such perplexities? Shall we say good-bye to Christian freedom, thus cutting off occasion for such dangers? But, as we have said, unless this freedom be comprehended, neither Christ nor gospel truth, not inner peace of soul, can be rightly known. Rather, we must take care that so necessary a part of doctrine be not suppressed, yet at the same time that those absurd objections which are wont to arise be met.
>
> (*Inst.* 3.19.1)

> *Quia simulatque iniecta est aliqua mentio Christianae libertatis, ibi aut fervent libidines, aut insani motus surgunt, nisi mature obviam eatur lascivis ingeniis istis, quae alioqui optima quaeque pessime corrumpunt. Partim enim huius libertatis praetextu omnem Dei obedientiam excutiunt, et in effraenatam licentiam se proripiunt: partim indignantur, putantes omnem moderationem, ordinem, rerumque delectum tolli. Quid hic agamus, talibus angustiis circunsepti? An Christiana libertate*

vaere iussa, huiusmodi periculis opportunitatem praecidamus? Atqui, ut dictum est, nisi ea tenetur, nec Christus, nec Evangelii veritas, neque interior pax animae recte cognoscitur. Danda potius opera ne adeo necessaria doctrinae pars supprimatur, et occurratur tamen interim absurdis illis obiectionibus quae inde enasci solent.
(*OS* 4:282.24–283.3)

Once again Calvin uses the rhetorical strategy of noting extremes and then setting out what seems to be a calm, moderate position. The extreme position here is represented by the anarchists, with whom he constantly battles to reclaim the idea of Christian freedom. Exegesis of this passage brings us back to the snapping heads of Scylla: in one case lusts or "passions boil" (*fervent libidines*); in another "wild tumults rise" (*insani motus surgunt*); in another we find licentious or "wanton spirits" (*lascivis ingeniis*), who pervert the best into the worst (*optima quaeque pessime corrumpunt*). Even more, they are disobedient and at the first opportunity "break out into unbridled license" (*effraenatam licentiam*), or they take things into their own hands and throw away all order and restraint. Now, for all Calvin's tendency to see more and more long necks with heads on them, they really come down to two: the individual abuse of freedom and a more political and collective one. I explore each one in some detail.

The terms in this passage tend to fall one way or another. Of course, it is true that a word like *libido* (we have the plural in this text) may have political overtones with its sense of pleasure and desire, but it tends strongly towards sensuality and lust—distinctly sexual and personal. So also with *lascivus*, which may mean playful or even flirtatious but far more commonly concerns what is lewd, lustful, or licentious. *Licentia* also joins the group, although more as a corrupted addition. Originally *licentia* meant freedom or liberty, if not permission (as in our license to drive or to sell alcohol), but soon enough it came to mean uncontrolled liberty or unbridled freedom. Just to make sure, Calvin adds *effraenatam*, which literally means "without rein" (as with a horse). And so we end up with a word that is close to our sense of license in a sexual and personal sense. What we have, then, with our trio of *libido, lascivis,* and *licentia*—a lascivious, licentious libido, if you will—is not merely alliteration but an image of the boiling lusts and swarming desires that can't wait to explode in an orgy.

By contrast a word like *insanus* is a little more ambiguous. Obviously the source of our "insane," it means not merely madness but also what is violent, outrageous, and excessive. Now, this could very well tend in the direction of political excess, which is where I will place it. After all, how often do we describe someone who takes a radical political stand as "eccentric" if not "mad"? Is it not far easier to place someone with the insane than take their political challenge seriously? I must admit that I have more than once been described as mad or "strange" in this way. Bicycle-riding and ship-traveling Marxist theologians are not, I must admit, part of the mainstream, at least in a country like Australia, which resembles the United States more and more. But in order to find some label for me, many relatives (blood relations, out-laws, and in-laws) find it easier to place me in the mad category. *Insanus* may be a little ambiguous. Not so the phrase "most wickedly corrupt the best things" (*optima quaeque pessime corrumpunt*). These people who misinterpret freedom want to corrupt, adulterate, or pervert (*corrumpo*) the best things (*optima*). Now, what these *optima* might be is never stated, so I will take *optima* as referring to the gospel and to society—in both cases something is spoiled as far as Calvin is concerned. Behind these phrases we can hear echoes of events that were still on everybody's minds, especially the radical Anabaptists of Münster, the placard wielders who came sneaking past the king of France's bedroom door, and the firebrand Thomas Müntzer and his peasant armies. Finally, the last phrase has a very similar import: "thinking that it takes away all moderation, order, and choice of things" (*putantes omnem moderationem, ordinem, rerumque delectum tolli*). The text speaks for itself.

Some terms seem to cover both the personal and the political. In our passage such an ambiguity is true of this phrase: "shake off all obedience toward God" (*omnem Dei obedientiam excutiunt*). These people cast or drive out (*excutio*) obedience to God, which may refer to what one does with one's carnal lusts or with one's political passions. Indeed, for Calvin the two are entwined: perverts, libertines, and sex addicts are also political rebels, and vice versa. Calvin has left quite a legacy here, for the two have been closely entwined at certain moments of political agitation. For example, the first stirrings of pornography with Aretino's *Sonnetti lussuriosi* of 1527 were tied up closely with political satire. And among the "grub street" presses of London in the eighteenth and nineteenth centuries, we find the same printers producing radical political tracts and pornographic texts.

Yet there is a reason for separating the two. Calvin is one of the first to express the relatively new attention to the private individual. He did not begin this process, for we can trace its checkered history back to Augustine's *Confessions*. Yet it always seems to play in a minor key, at least until Calvin's time. The fact that Augustine is a favorite of Calvin probably helped, but there was something else in the air. Call it epochal change, the collapse of feudalism and the first stirrings of capitalism, an awakening of the spirit, religious revival—but there was something new. A major feature of this seismic shift is the new concern with the individual. Now it is *my* feelings, my personal beliefs and acts, my body, and my democratic rights that first begin to awaken. And Calvin gave them a good kick along.

Marx was one of the first to point to such a change through one of his favorite figures, Martin Luther (in fact, Marx sometimes saw himself as a second Luther). Here he is:

> Luther, we grant, overcame the bondage of piety by replacing it by the bondage of conviction. He shattered faith in authority because he restored the authority of faith. He turned priests into laymen because he turned laymen into priests. He freed man from outer religiosity because he made religiosity the inner man. He freed the body from chains because he enchained the heart.
> (Marx 1975, 182)

Here is a fundamental shift from external to internal religiosity. Against all forms of outer religiosity—piety, authority, priests, and the body—he pressed for the internalization of religious commitment, one characterized by conviction, faith, laity, and the heart of the inner man. This internalization, or as I prefer, privatization, becomes the huge step forward. All the same, Marx's description is a backhanded compliment. The first and last sentences in the quotation from Marx bring it out all too clearly: Luther might have freed people from external religious forms, but he brought about a whole new level of enslavement—that of conviction and the heart.

Michel Foucault was to pick up this point and make it central to his *Discipline and Punish* (1979). Here he is interested in the way public, brutal, and very bloody forms of punishment—the stock, public torture, or execution—gave way to private and internalized forms. The issue then becomes one of private punishment, the search for motive and intention in crime, the desire for moral reform, and so on. He also traces the way surveillance becomes crucial, including surveillance of the soul.

All of this is very pertinent to Calvin. Indeed the comment first applied to Luther also sums up Calvin: "He freed man from outer religiosity because he made religiosity the inner man" (Marx 1975, 182). Once you have built this new internal private space, with its brand-new furniture and knickknacks, what happens to the old space where everyone used to gather and share things? It becomes the public space. What you can do there also changes. Spectacles of punishment start to disappear, but so do celebrations of sex, food, and drink—that is, the old carnival. In short, what used to be the major focus of human existence, namely, the collective life of a town or village, now becomes the space where you can engage in politics.

Calvin was very keen on this separation, for it gave him an extremely useful device for blocking the radical readings of Christian liberty. More specifically, he needs to make a sharp break between the private and the public in order to avoid the political consequences of his doctrine of Christian liberty. As he puts it, "But we must carefully note that Christian freedom is, in all its parts, *a spiritual matter* [*Christianam libertatem omnibus suis partibus rem spiritualem esse*]" (*Inst.* 3.19.9; *OS* 4:288.15–16; translation modified and emphasis added). More extensively:

> Therefore, in order that none of us may stumble on that stone, let us first consider that there is a twofold government in man: one aspect is spiritual, whereby the conscience is instructed in piety and in reverencing God; the second is political, whereby man is educated for the duties of humanity and citizenship that must be maintained among men. These are usually called the "spiritual" and the "temporal" jurisdiction (not improper terms) by which is meant that the former sort of government pertains to the life of the soul, while the latter has to do with the concerns of the present life—not only with food and clothing but with laying down laws whereby a man may live his life among other men holily, honorably, and temperately. For the former resides in the inner mind, while the latter regulates only outward behavior. The one we may call the spiritual kingdom, the other, the political kingdom. Now these two, as we have divided them, must always be examined separately; and while one is being considered, we must call away and turn aside the mind from thinking about the other. There are in man, so to speak, two worlds, over which different kings and different laws have authority.
>
> Through this distinction it comes about that we are not to misapply to the political order the gospel teaching on spiritual freedom, as if Christians were less subject, as concerns outward government, to human laws, because their consciences have been set free in God's sight; as if they were released from all bodily servitude because they are free according to the spirit.
>
> Then, because there can be some delusion in the constitutions that seem to apply to the spiritual kingdom, among these also we should

discern what must be considered lawful, as consonant with God's word, and on the other hand what ought to have no place among the godly. Of civil government we shall speak in another place.
(*Inst.* 3.19.15; *OS* 4:294.4–31)

This is an astounding passage, worthy of closer attention. First, an astute reader will have noticed that the two long quotations in this section come from either end of the nineteenth chapter of the third book of the *Institutes*. Both speak of a private spiritual realm and a public temporal one, although the latter one does so more clearly. What we have in fact is a case of literary chiasm, where similar themes or thoughts recur in mirrorlike structural positions. So the private-public split opens and closes the chapter, while its bulk speaks of the three types of freedom. In other words, Calvin has unwittingly boxed in the most radical section of his chapter by the private-public distinction.

Second, there is something peculiar about the quotation above. Initially I intended to quote the key points of this section, but as it went along, I realized Calvin was repeating himself over and over again. All he says is that we need to distinguish as sharply as possible between the spiritual and temporal senses of Christian liberty. He could have said so in one sentence. So why say it so many times?

The answer is that this is a deeply traumatic point for him. I count nine repetitions of the same basic point, coming to its sharpest expression in this sentence: "Through this distinction it comes about that we are not to misapply to the political order the gospel teaching on spiritual freedom." One of Freud's basic arguments concerning obsessive repetition is that it marks the failure to resolve a trauma, a failure to work it through and achieve some sort of normal existence. Such compulsive repetition may be an effort to ward off the trauma, such as found in war victims, or it may be an attempt to repeat the traumatic event or its circumstances over and over again in order to gain some control over it. One might "relive" the event in dreams or believe that by repeating the story of what happened, one can ward off the trauma. Freud's famous example in his 1920 essay "Beyond the Pleasure Principle" ([1920] 2001) is of his grandson Ernst. Freud observed that Ernst used to throw his favorite toy from his crib, become upset at the loss, then reel the toy back, only to repeat this action again and again and again. All the while the child cried "o-o-o-o" and "da," which Freud translates as "*fort-da*," "gone-there." It is an easy game to play, watching a small child throw a toy out of reach and then cry for it to be retrieved. Freud suggests that the little boy in question would play the game repeatedly when his mother was absent, thereby using the toy as a surrogate for his mother. The trauma in question was an absent mother; the repetition was the game with the toy.

Such traumas take many shapes. For example, the face of unspeakable horror in war may leave one with permanent psychological scars. A veteran may not be able to eat rice ever again because the individual grains are an all-too-ready reminder of maggots in wounds of the living. Or perhaps missing a crucial event such as the funeral of one's father may generate an obsession with time. Yet no matter how often the person in question checks a watch or a clock, he or she always ends up being late.

I would suggest that the trauma for Calvin is that he can see a very radical seed within the doctrine of Christian freedom. He recognizes that such a seed appears quite clearly in the Epistle to the Galatians (*Inst.* 3.19.3; *OS* 4:283.34–284.27). Yet everything within him rebels at the thought that the gospel of Jesus Christ would lead in this direction. On top of this is yet another trauma: the Peasants' War of 1525, the Münster Revolution, and the Placards Affair had scarred his soul. These revolutionaries had, after all, claimed the Bible for themselves and read the script for their revolutionary activity out of that same text. But I would suggest a yet deeper trauma that constantly lurks in the *Institutes*: that God may well be speaking multivocally and not univocally, that he may be condoning the radical political freedoms that Calvin sets his heart to block. Everywhere he turns he seems to face that problem of a radical, multivocal God, even in the midst of his own arguments. It appears when he argues that the Christian is freed from the law to serve Christ, when he states that all external observances are of no consequence, and when he suggests that Christians are beholden to human laws on these matters. But then he sees the danger and takes deep fright. At that moment he slams the gate shut and claims that such an idea of freedom applies only to the spiritual, private life of the Christian. It has nothing to do, he argues, with the public, temporal realm of civil government.

THE PARADOX OF CALVINIST LEGALISM

In all this discussion of Christian freedom, the difficulties Calvin has in negotiating Scylla and Charybdis, the desperate effort to curtail freedom and its tendency to slip out of his hands, there is a nagging question: Why does Calvinism all too often descend into legalism? This is a very personal question as well.

I recall all too well the ban on television on a Sunday, the Lord's Day of rest: by watching it we were tacitly approving the fact that those people on TV were working. And certainly no one should work on a Sunday. Or if one of us (there were five children) wanted to slip off to the shop on a Sunday, then he or she would be told in no uncertain terms that buying and selling were out on that day of the week. If we were on holidays, which involved a monthlong camping trip in a small car with seven people and a dog, moving from place to place like nomads or gypsies, then we would not travel on the first day of the week, except to get to some remote church, where we tripled the attendance. Team sports were never encouraged, but when my brothers began to play different codes of football, they were banned from playing on that day. One notorious event involved my father hiding my brother's football boots before he was due to go on a weekend gala trip. Next time my brother didn't say anything and disappeared. All hell broke loose. Needless to say, my brother has not really come to terms with such treatment. But the one that sticks in my mind, especially as one who loved to read and write from an early age, was the constant surveillance to see if any one of us was studying on a Sunday. That too was work. Even if I had an exam on Monday, or perhaps an essay due, I was told that I should have been more organized and studied or finished the essay before Sunday. Even now, when my parents visit and find me reading some heavy tome or perhaps sitting at my writing desk, or if I say that I have been to the shops to get some food for their visit, it is as though I have pressed "play"—the warning I have heard a million times before it gets rolled out once again. Of course, mentioning the story of the disciples eating ears of wheat while crossing a field on the Sabbath always produced a stern reprimand, as did the one about Jesus healing on the Sabbath and having to face up to a grilling from his learned opponents.

The greatest sin, even worse than the sin against the Holy Spirit, was to miss church. No effort or expense was spared. No matter if we were stuck in the middle of the Great Sandy Desert of Central Australia, we would find a church. Even if it involved driving all day to some remote mountain village, we would find a church. While camping, we had a special suitcase with "Sunday clothes," which would be retrieved ceremoniously on a Sunday morning, and after a good scrubbing, we would all be decked out and lined up in the front pew. No matter if the preacher was atrocious, the singing a harbinger of the wails of hell, and the church gutted by termites, we would go. And if there was no church building, my father would organize his own service. I recall one Sunday in the deserts of western New South Wales when he placed a notice on the toilet doors of the rough camping area, and a few stragglers turned up. Then my father sat on a camp stool beneath a large tree and read from his battered Bible, led the prayers in his usual somber "forgive-us-all-our-sins" style, and offered a sermon that he had scribbled on the back of some toilet paper or spare tent canvas. "Remember the Lord's Day, to keep it holy" was a rule that must *not* under any circumstances be broken.

No surprise, then, that we developed all manner of subterfuges. Television might have been a bit tricky, but the trip to the shops was much easier to pull off (under cover of playing with friends), and one could always hide that textbook within another one, sit on the lounge, and seem to be relaxing. Even now, although I have moved beyond the feeling of freedom that came from not attending church when I chose, writing on a Sunday gives me that small thrill of rebellion.

It was this outward manifestation of Calvinism that I rejected for many years. I explored Pelagianism, Christian humanism, asserted the role of free will, and sided with Erasmus over against Luther on the matter, and so on. The reason: my experience at the level of everyday life was that Calvinism was a system of oppressive rules and regulations. It was best to be well and truly rid of it.

Eventually my simplistic rejection and rebellion took another shape. I began to sense a profound contradiction within my Reformed upbringing: Why does Christian liberty in Calvin's hands turn into bondage to rules and regulations? Why does a theological system that has justification by faith through grace at its core have such a tendency to become legalistic? In short, why does grace end up with the law?

The answers to these questions all come back to Calvin himself, especially the brave effort to make his run between a rock and a hard place, between Scylla and Charybdis. On a number of occasions now, we have seen him work very hard to avoid the radical heads of Scylla and their "misinterpretations" of Christian liberty. Such freedom is central to the gospel, Calvin argues, but then he tries to specify precisely what freedom is. It is freedom from the law and freedom for Christ; freedom from outer compulsion and for inner desire; and freedom from the observance of those unnecessary and indifferent external items that really boil down to nothing more than superstitions. Nice and neat, is it not? Three types of freedom neatly defined. I can imagine Calvin leaning back from his writing desk, dusting his hands in satisfaction, and thinking, That should do it! That should keep those rabid radicals from misinterpreting Christian freedom. But then he jumps. Oh my God! Freedom from the law and for Christ and freedom according to one's inner compulsion is like political gunpowder. So Calvin hurriedly returns to his manuscript and introduces that crucial distinction between spiritual and temporal, between private and public. Such freedom is fine for the private, inner, spiritual life, where one is freed from the law of faith. But it does not apply to the external, temporal life that we experience in this world. And just in case freedom should escape in the structure of the chapter, he surrounds it with the public-private distinction in a literary chiasm.

So freedom has been boxed in, limited to the individual's own inner life with God—what we have come to call the life of faith. We must, as Calvin puts it so well, "descend into ourselves (*ad nos . . . descendere*)" (*Inst.* 2.8.3; *OS* 3:345.15–16).[5] At this point, a critical reader may well object, That is all very well. Calvin has carefully clipped freedom's wings, but within that space Christian liberty is free to do as it pleases. His distinction between the spiritual and the temporal still leaves freedom to run its course in the spiritual realm. Boxed in it might be, argues my imaginary critic, but it can still pace around in its tiny inner courtyard. To be blunt, even with those restrictions, freedom is still free to be itself. One is still free from the law. In response, I would argue that this is a false move. A restricted freedom is a strange one indeed. It is as though a prison guard were to say to a prisoner, You have absolute freedom, but only within these walls and during the times that we set down. In the very act of erecting such restrictions, Calvin reenacts the whole problem of the law, precisely the one that he seeks to overcome. What are such restrictions but the return of laws that set boundaries and sanctions to the exercise of freedom? It is though he is saying, Sure, you can have freedom, but only according to the rules that I lay down.[6]

Charybdis's whirlpool is starting to suck at the edges of Calvin's craft. . . .

---

5. See also his discussion of confession as an inner process addressed to God alone (*Inst.* 3.4.9–12; *OS* 4:95–99).
6. He certainly has a love of expounding on the law; see especially the extraordinarily long chapter on the Ten Commandments (*Inst.* 2.8; *OS* 3:343–98). Needless to say, I resist Stevenson's (1999) desire to seek a bland resolution through responsible freedom.

5
Politics
Overthrowing Ungodly Rulers

In the final chapter of the *Institutes*—book 4, chapter 20, to be precise—the theological rubber hits the political road. In this treatment "Of Civil Government [*De Politica Administatione*]," Calvin squares up to politics or what he sometimes calls the "temporal" realm. Every sentence of this chapter manifests the tension I have been tracing throughout this book: Calvin sees the radical possibilities that the Bible can show from time to time, and he tries to contain it within his own careful boundaries only for it to break out again.[1] Or if we return to our revolutionary cat, the question now is whether our feline friend finally breaks through the small hole Calvin has given him or whether Calvin manages to tie the bag up once and for all.

I begin with the crucial paragraph of the whole chapter, bring out its main points, and then retrace the steps by which Calvin arduously works his way towards this paragraph.

> But in that obedience which we have shown to be due the authority of rulers, we are always to make this exception, indeed, to observe it as primary, that such obedience is never to lead us away from obedience

---

1. Structurally, too, there is something amiss with the chapter. It seems as though he couldn't quite get on top of the material. Calvin sets out in this last chapter of the *Institutes* to speak of three categories: the magistrate, the laws, and the people (*Inst.* 4.20.3; *OS* 5:474.17–24). Yet before too long, kings turn up, so that we find a competing structure: king, magistrate (and the laws), and people. One is the ostensible structure of his chapter, while the other of the political reality with which he tries to deal. They are at odds with each other, clashing from time to time, all of which suggests an inability to control what is happening with the discussion. See further Stevenson (1999, 32–36; 2004), Bousma (1988, 204–13), Steinmetz (1995, 199–208), and Willis-Watkins (1989).

to him, to whose will the desires of all kings ought to be subject, to whose decrees all their commands ought to yield, to whose majesty their scepters ought to be submitted. And how absurd would it be that in satisfying men you should incur the displeasure of him for whose sake you obey men themselves! The Lord, therefore, is the King of kings, who, when he has opened his sacred mouth, must alone be heard before all and above all men; next to him we are subject to those men who are in authority over us, but only in him. If they command anything against him, let it go unesteemed. And here let us not be concerned about all that dignity which the magistrates possess, for no harm is done to it when it is humbled before that singular and truly supreme power of God.
(*Inst.* 4.20.32; *OS* 5:501.28–502.3)

To my mind, nothing could be clearer. If a ruler goes against the commands of God, then we have no need to obey the ruler. When it comes to a choice between obedience to God or obedience to an ungodly ruler, there is no choice. We may be subject to those who rule over us, but "subject only in the Lord." So, writes Calvin, "if they command anything against him, let it go unesteemed," or as the translation by Beveridge has, "let us not pay the least regard to it." I will have more to say about this extraordinary paragraph at the end of my discussion, so let us leave it for now and trace our way back to the beginning of the last chapter of the *Institutes*.

FROM SEPARATION TO ENTANGLEMENT

Through this long and winding chapter, Calvin tries to negotiate three main tensions: between the temporal and the spiritual; between tyranny and anarchy; and then between obedience to evil rulers and obedience to God. The last one is the most interesting for this book (and obviously the subject of the paragraph I have quoted above), but let us take the argument one point at a time.

We have already encountered Calvin's sharp distinction between the spiritual and the temporal in my treatment of Christian freedom (see chapter 3). In a last-ditch effort to block the argument that Christian liberty—as liberty from the law through the grace of Christ—has radical political potential, Calvin slams into place the distinction between spiritual and temporal. Such liberty from the law and for Christ, he argues, applies only to the spiritual domain. Temporally, one is subject to all the laws of the land. One is free only in that private, inner zone, in the inner life of faith.

The opening comments in the last chapter of the *Institutes* begin on a similar note. Of the "two governments" within us, Calvin admits that he has spent most of his energy exploring the inner one, which relates directly to eternal life, but that he does indeed need to say a few things about the other one, "which pertains only to the establishment of justice and outward morality" (*Inst.* 4.20.1; *OS* 5:471.15–16). Here, too, he asserts the sharp difference between them for the same reasons as he did in his earlier discussion of "Christian freedom": it is to forestall those sadly mistaken souls who think that the promise of liberty from the law relates to this fleeting, temporal realm. These characters seek to overcome all that interferes with their freedom in this life—laws, courts, magistrates, and what have you—until the revolution has been achieved, or as he puts it, "unless the whole world is reformed into a new form [*nisi totus in novam faciem orbis reformetur*]" (*Inst.* 4.20.1; *OS* 5:472.11–12; translation modified). Not so fast, Calvin points out, for the spiritual and the temporal are poles apart and simply cannot be confused with one another.

Spiritual is spiritual and temporal is temporal, and never the twain shall meet. Or so it would seem: as soon as he has reasserted his earlier argument, Calvin switches tack. Despite this very sharp separation between the realms, Calvin goes on to write, "We must know that they do not contend with each other [*ita nec quicquam pugnare sciendum est*]" (*Inst.* 4.20.2; *OS* 5:473.8–9; my translation). *Pugnare* is a strong word, meaning fight, struggle, and contend. The spiritual and temporal realms do not battle with each other; they are not opposed. Distinct but not opposed—it is a neat distinction. And it appears a minor concession, a small point in a larger argument. Yet it is extraordinarily important: now the spiritual and temporal, the internal and external, are in fact connected. Much turns on this concession, for once Calvin admits that the spiritual and temporal are in fact connected, a mass of items floods in (see Graham 1978, 158–59).

So what role does a civil government have in the life of faith? For starters, it should ban idolatry, blasphemy, and any slanders against the truth (*Inst.* 4.20.3; *OS* 5:473.30–474.24). That is substantial enough, but Calvin goes on to suggest that such government might also maintain public peace and quiet, and perhaps ensure that private property remains intact (a good early capitalist line). While we are on the topic, why not include the protection of commerce, as well as ways of maintaining honesty and modesty and even a decent form of public religion among Christians? A rather comprehensive list, is it not? I cannot help thinking of that initial list of revolutionary elements in the preface, where Calvin tries to reassure Francis I of France that he and his cronies are not in the business of overthrowing the laws and the courts, disturbing the peace, tearing scepters from the hand of kings, or to sum it up, turning society upside down. Here he comes through as a good conservative: everything must be done to ensure that order is maintained and no revolutionary threat can arise. But he has gone much further than such conservatism, for the proper task of government is to protect and nurture "the true religion [*vera religio*] which is contained in God's law" (*Inst.* 4.20.3; *OS* 5.474.13; see also *Inst.* 4.20.9; *OS* 5:479–81). If it does so, then the very earthly civil government actually plays a role like that of food and water, even light and air, albeit with greater dignity.

I have been giving an exposition of the third paragraph of chapter 20 because it brings out how closely the spiritual and the temporal realms have come in the space of a few short sentences. But Calvin realizes that his argument seems like a complete about-face, so he sets out to show why it isn't. As a first step to exploring that difficult task, I need to ask a question: Why does he make such a move to connect the spiritual and temporal? The short answer is that he wants to prevent both tyranny and anarchy. The long answer is in what follows.

BETWEEN ANARCHY AND TYRANNY

This opposition between tyranny and anarchy is one of the structuring features of the whole chapter. Initially, Calvin deals with various forms of anarchy, whether spiritual escapism or political radicalism. Later, he focuses on tyranny, working away at the problem of what Christians should do when faced with ungodly rulers. Let me take each one in turn.

We have already met political radicalism a few times, especially in its anarchistic form. What happens here is that the spiritual and temporal are connected very closely. Disdain for the existing political order, the law, and other grubby matters of human society translates into a radical and anarchistic agenda. The social, economic, and political life of this world is corrupt and depraved. However, instead of retreating from it, they seek to overthrow and replace it with a properly holy society. In what is a rather good description of anarchism, Calvin writes,

"They . . . think that nothing will be safe unless the whole world is reshaped to a new form, where there are neither courts, nor laws, nor magistrates, nor anything, which in their opinion restricts their freedom" (*Inst.* 4.20.1; *OS* 5:472.10–13). Faced with such a close connection between the spiritual and the temporal in the hands of such anarchists, Calvin opts for their separation—at least in this instance.

Spiritual escapism is a relatively new beast, although its crux is the radical separation of spiritual and temporal. It may take two forms. On the one hand, it is a retreat within when faced with the troubled and complex matters of the world. I may find a quiet corner away from the cares and worries of life, block them out as best I can, and live my inner life of faith in peaceful solitude. On the other hand, it may mean a complete disdain of the things of this world. Since we already have one foot in heaven and sit at the table of the Lord, we really don't need to bother with the laws and sanctions of society. We are far above all those messy earthly matters and can therefore ignore the grubby matters of politics and the legal system. We are, in short, a law unto ourselves; or rather, we already live out God's law and need no law of men. Both types of spiritual escapism are problematic for Calvin (see *Inst.* 4.20.2; *OS* 5:472.35–473.29). He knows full well that his argument for the purely spiritual and inner domain of Christian faith can lead in this direction, so in this case he switches and seeks to connect both spiritual and temporal.

In the remainder of this last chapter of the *Institutes*, Calvin keeps both forms of anarchy in mind: to counter the political anarchists, he constantly asserts the need to obey one's earthly rulers since they have been appointed by God; against the spiritual escapists, he harps on the point that civil government is there to protect and nurture the life of faith. But it is really tyranny that draws more and more of his attention.

Already in his opening statement, Calvin lays out the threat of absolute power. Although he speaks of finding a way between the two extremes of anarchy and tyranny—between the "insane and barbarous men" trying to overthrow God's order (our political anarchists) and the "flatterers of princes" who oppose God's government by praising the princes' earthly "power without measure [*potentiam sine modo*]" (*Inst.* 4.20.1; *OS* 5:471.21–23)—he is actually more interested in countering tyranny. And the nub of the problem is that if an earthly ruler is opposed to God, what is a Christian or indeed a citizen to do?

The answer is not clear. For a man given to a near-obsessive precision and the careful arrangement of his arguments, this is curious indeed. Something must be bugging him. In fact, Calvin resorts to his usual efforts to categorize and organize. So we find that most of his attention in this last chapter is given over to the respective roles of the king, magistrate, laws, and people. This time his famed precision does not help him. One would imagine that the simple question—what to do with an ungodly ruler?—would be relatively easy to answer. But not so, and the reason is that Calvin is far too good a student of the Bible to find an easy answer to the question. So let us follow him through as he twists and turns.

WHAT TO DO WITH AN UNGODLY RULER

In section after section (from the fourth to the thirteenth of chapter 20) we find various tasks of the rulers, both kings and magistrates. Calvin begins by emphasizing that they are appointed by God (*Inst.* 4.20.4–7; *OS* 5:474.25–478.10) but then already raises the problem of what to do when they tend towards tyranny. His preliminary response is to argue for a small aristocracy bordering on popular government (*Inst.* 4.20.8; *OS* 5:478.11–479.31) in order keep tyranny in check. Here his theology meshes with his politics very closely: In the same way that he has a democracy of depravity and an aristocracy of salvation, Calvin argues for an aristocratic government with distinct popular elements. Because monarchy tends towards tyranny, aristocracy slips all too easily towards the faction of the few, and because popular government has a knack of being seditious, he seeks a system with the proverbial checks and balances: "Therefore, men's fault or failing causes it to be safer and more bearable for a number to exercise government, so that they may help one another, teach and admonish one another; and, if one asserts himself unfairly, there may be a number of censors and masters to restrain his willfulness" (*Inst.* 4.20.8; *OS* 5:478.28–479.2). No democrat here: rather, he is a careful conservative who feels that the Bible points in this direction. But he is also not about to plunge into arguments for absolute monarchy, for this would be an open ticket to the exercise of excessive power and tyranny. Once again his admirable effort to specify two extremes and then walk a line between them shows itself. His position seems so reasonable, the strategy so persuasive, that I can't help but nod in agreement.

The next few sections cover matters such as the close relation between spiritual and temporal laws (*Inst.* 4.20.9; *OS* 5:479.32–481.26), an effort to find a moderate position between the command not to kill and the need for the death penalty (*Inst.* 4.20.10; *OS* 5:481.27–483.28), as well as the uses of war in light of the same argument and the need to keep sedition in check (*Inst.* 4.20.11–12; *OS* 5:483.28–485.17). Taxes (*Inst.* 4.20.13; *OS* 5:485.18–486.8) should also be necessary but not tyrannical. And then we dip into a lengthy discussion of the law (*Inst.* 4.20.14–21; *OS* 5:486.9–493.15), where Calvin argues that the basis of civil law is and should be Moses' law and not some common law. We are a long way indeed from that sharp division between temporal and spiritual realms on which Calvin was so keen not that long ago. In fact, here he goes so far as to argue that revelation is the basis of temporal law!

I have outlined all too briefly some features of Calvin's effort to give precise order to matters pertaining to civil government. Although the threat of anarchy turns up every now and then—especially on the dangers of popular government—we really gain the sense that it is not the major issue. That sense is enhanced when we come to the closing sections of the chapter, for this is where Calvin really comes to grips with the issue of tyranny. And he is driven to do so by a series of (for him) difficult biblical texts that deal with the overthrow of a ruler.

Obedience

Calvin begins the final stages of this chapter by asserting the importance of obedience to divinely appointed rulers. Starting with the flagship text of Romans 13:1–2, he brings out a string of biblical texts to show that this is as solid a biblical position as one will find: Titus 3:1 on obeying the powers, principalities, and magistrates; 1 Peter 2:13 on submission to kings and governors; 1 Timothy 2:1–2 on prayers and intercessions for all in authority (*Inst.* 4.20.23; *OS* 5:494.6–26).[2]

Well and good, one might want to say. The Bible has plenty of texts that give divine sanction to the ruler, whether king, dictator, or despot. And over the last two millennia there have been more than enough rulers and small-minded churchmen who have been all too ready to use such texts for their own megalomaniac programs. So we face our next problem: if the Bible says we must obey our rulers, what do we do with the dreary run of ungodly and tyrannical ones? Calvin's initial answer is, as we might expect, rather conservative:

---

2. Stevenson (1999, 143–44; 2004) heavily stresses this element in Calvin's political thought, drawing on letters that give direct advice on the matter. See also the commentaries on 1 Pet. 2:13 (Calvin 1855, 79–80), 1 Tim. 2:1–2 (Calvin 1856, 51–3), and Titus 3:1 (Calvin 1856, 324).

> Indeed, he says that those who rule for the public benefit are true patterns and evidences of this beneficence of his; that they who rule unjustly and incompetently have been raised up by him to punish the wickedness of the people; that all equally have been endowed with that holy majesty with which he has invested lawful power.
> (*Inst.* 4.20.25; *OS* 5:470.1–6)[3]

At this point Calvin takes the line that such a ruler is still to be obeyed, since he may be an agent of punishment in God's hands. The worst tyrant is still in a divinely appointed role, even if it is to remind us of our sinful state. Now, it would be a stretch to imagine a president or prime minister in our own time arguing that she or he has been sent by God to punish us. Then again, many have often felt precisely this way—that their elected ruler has been sent to punish them for one or other unknown sin. I am sure that most readers would be able to identify at least one ruler they have experienced personally who fits Calvin's colorful description:

> If we are cruelly tormented by a savage prince, if we are greedily despoiled by one who is avaricious or wanton, if we are neglected by a slothful one, if finally we are vexed for piety's sake by one who is impious and sacrilegious, let us first be mindful of our own misdeeds, which without doubt are chastised by such whips of the Lord.
> (*Inst.* 4.20.29; *OS* 5:499.33–500.2)

So the first proposition is in place: the people must not disobey or even contemplate removing an ungodly ruler, no matter how rapacious or outrageous he (or at times she) might be. This would be an excellent place to close his argument, especially for a conservative like Calvin. It would also enable him to take his place beside Luther, forming a solid line on the question of the two kingdoms.

God and Agents

The problem is that Calvin is too good a student of the Bible. For in that troublesome text he finds at least two situations when one may remove a ruler from power. However, that "one" is not anyone: only God may do so or someone specifically appointed by God for that

---

3. So also, "When we hear that a king has been ordained by God, let us at once call to mind those heavenly edicts with regard to honoring and fearing a king; then we shall not hesitate to hold a most wicked tyrant in the place where the Lord has deigned to set him" (*Inst.* 4.20.26; *OS* 5:497.10–13).

purpose, whether such a person knows he or she has been given this desirable task or not. As for the first category, God's wrath has been and will be directed at any ruler who happens to disobey God. In language that comes all too close to the Hebrew prophets and even (God forbid!) the likes of Thomas Müntzer, Calvin writes,

> Before his face all kings shall fall and be crushed, and all the judges of the earth, that have not kissed his anointed [Ps. 2:10-11], and all those who have written unjust laws to oppress the poor in judgment and to do violence to the cause of the lowly, to prey upon widows and rob the fatherless [Isa. 10:1-2].
> (*Inst.* 4.20.29; *OS* 5:500.7-13)

This is a rather important text, for it is both saturated in biblical allusions and marks the emergence of a different position on ungodly rulers.[4] And the crucial principle that swings into action here is as follows: rulers are not different from anyone else, so if they have done wrong, they deserve to be punished for it. All have sinned and fallen short of the glory of God—and that includes rulers. In case the odd anarchist might start to get excited, with fingers twitching at the scabbard, Calvin makes it perfectly clear that this task of removing an ungodly ruler is strictly God's . . . unless of course he happens to appoint someone to do the dirty work for him:

> Here are revealed his goodness, his power, and his providence. For sometimes he raises up open avengers [*vindices*] from among his servants, and arms them with his command to punish [*poenas sumant*] the accursed tyranny and deliver [*eximant*] his people, oppressed in unjust ways, from miserable calamity. Sometimes he directs to this end the rage of men with other intentions and other endeavors. . . . For the first kind of men, when they had been sent by God's lawful calling to carry out such acts, in taking up arms [*arma sumendo*] against kings, did not at all violate that majesty which is implanted in kings by God's ordination; but armed from heaven, they subdued [*coercebant*] the lesser power with the greater, just as it is lawful for kings to punish [*animadvertere*] their subordinates. But the latter kind of men, although they were directed by God's hand whither he pleased, and executed his work unwittingly, yet planned in their minds to do nothing but an evil act.
> (*Inst.* 4.20.30; *OS* 5:500.14-19, 29-501.4)

---

4. The allusions are to Ps. 2:10 and Isa. 10:1. We can see such a position espoused quite clearly in his commentaries on these passages (Calvin 1845, 22-24; 1850, 333-34).

There are in fact two types of agent in the divine (secret) service of doing away with sundry rulers or at least delivering the people from the iron fist of impious oppression. Perhaps the best way to distinguish them is in terms of the conscious/unconscious distinction. Some are directly appointed for the task, perfectly conscious of the role assigned to them (however unwilling they might be), and undertake this ministry with more or less gusto. The examples are easy to call to mind (I cull a few from Calvin and add a few others): Moses and the ungodly rule of Pharaoh; Gideon and freedom from Midianite oppression; Othniel the judge who overthrew the oppression of Cushan-rishathaim, the king of Mesopotamia; Ehud the judge and assassin of Eglon king of Moab; Esther and Mordecai in response to the oppression of Haman; and so on.

However, others are not conscious of their divinely appointed roles and are co-opted into the task without their knowledge. In fact, they may think that some minor affront needs to be avenged and may be driven by fury and evil intent, but still they carry out the divine purpose (see also *Inst.* 1.18; *OS* 3:219–27). The biblical examples are not as numerous on this count, but we can find them nonetheless. The most notable of these is Cyrus, king of the Medes and Persians, who is named by Isaiah as Yahweh's anointed—"messiah," no less, in Isaiah 45:1 (see Calvin 1852c, 394–95). Others include the use of one state to punish another—Tyre is punished by Egypt, but then Egypt is punished in turn by the Assyrians, who in their turn are chastised by the Babylonians, and they get their own medicine from the Medes and Persians (under our friend Cyrus). Not a bad way to read the processes of imperial rise and fall, but then Calvin also points out that these empires punish Israel and Judah with sickening regularity.

But note carefully what has happened with this move by Calvin. Two fascinating twists have appeared in his argument, the first explicitly recognized by Calvin, the second not. The first of these is one of the many moments when he sets out to reconcile what is really a contradiction: God appoints rulers (and so we must obey them), but then God also appoints agents to restrain (*coerceo*), punish (*animadverto*), inflict recompense on (*poenas sumo*), take up arms against (*arma sumo*), and deliver from (*eximo*) ungodly rulers. How to make sense of this contradiction? Calvin asserts that such agents "did not at all violate that majesty which is implanted in kings by God's ordination." How so? Another order now comes into play. The people may be commanded to obey rulers appointed by God, but those rulers must obey the one who appointed them in the first place. They might be kings, but God is

King of kings. Or as Calvin puts it, they are his subordinates or satraps (*satrapas*). The catch with this argument, which was initially produced to deal with a biblical contradiction, is that it introduces a further problem for Calvin: rulers need to obey God. If they do not, they may well be punished. The emergence of this position will lead us eventually to the explosive conclusion to chapter 20.

The second argument concerning these divine agents of political vengeance—that God may use for his own good the evil intent of others—introduces an argument fraught with danger. It may go in either direction. For instance, I can see it being used by some for the argument that Hitler actually carried out a good and necessary task despite his evil intent, namely, the belated bourgeois revolution in Germany. But then it may also be used to argue that Stalin, however brutal he might have been, did succeed in modernizing Russia. Or indeed, that China's annexation of Tibet has brought it into the modern world, or that the theft of Hawaii by the United States has been good for the place in the long run. The list is endless, but it boils down to the old Jesuit position that the end justifies the means. Adding the qualifier that the good in question must be good for God's people does not change the volatility of the original point. To my mind it is an extraordinarily dangerous line to take.

We have reached the end of the second turn in Calvin's argument. At first we found him asserting, with the assistance of a long list of texts, that the ruler must be obeyed even if he is an oppressive, evil, and ungodly ruler. But then Calvin had to come to terms with those biblical texts that tell stories about punishing or removing ungodly rulers, so he allows that either God or one of his agents may avenge or punish a wayward and tyrannical ruler—a position fraught with dangers.

Magistrate

Now for the third turn of his argument—the magistrate. This crucial figure actually fills a gap. When I first read Calvin's text on the divinely appointed agent whose task it is to curb and punish ungodly rulers, I began to wonder why the ministry of removing such rulers has not made it into the regular ordained ministries of the church. I pondered what the theological training for such a ministry would entail and how one might construct an ordination service. But then I realized that it has become a ministry of sorts—in the form of the magistrate (*magistratus*).

But who is the magistrate? In Calvin's text the magistrate is the contemporary form taken by the divinely appointed agent whose task (in part) is to curb the tyrannical excesses of the king. In this respect the magistrate occupies an intermediate position between king and people. Calvin sees such a magistrate embodied in figures like Moses, who receives the law from God and appoints seventy judges to manage the judicial load (Exod. 18:13–27; see Calvin 1852b, 302–12), or like the judges in the book of the same name in the Hebrew Bible, or Samuel in the books of his name. Indeed, a little earlier Calvin is drawn to the texts of 1 Samuel, although he uses them to point out that the people should obey an unjust king (1 Sam. 8:11–17) and then to show how even David refrained from taking Saul's life when he had Saul in his power (1 Sam. 24). Yet Samuel the judge or magistrate functions at another level here, for he is the one who both anoints and removes kings from office. Though Samuel anoints Saul as the first king of Israel, he later removes that divine sanction from Saul and transfers it to David. This king-making magistrate is one who seems to have played a role in Calvin's depiction of the relations between magistrate and king.

As far as the historical situation in Calvin's own time is concerned, the magistrate was not merely a bureaucrat or even a law clerk, as we tend to think of magistrates now. Their task was to watch over public affairs, keep a watch on other public officials, collect taxes, lead armies into battle if need be, execute the odd criminal as a last resort, and of course, see that the laws were followed and enforced. It should be no surprise, then, that Calvin covers these topics in this last chapter.

One of the tasks of the magistrate is that he has been "appointed to restrain [*ad moderandam*] the wantonness [*libidinem*] of kings." And just to make sure, Calvin repeats the comment in a slightly different way: magistrates are appointed "to withstand [*intercedere*], in accordance with their duty, the fierce licentiousness [*licentiae*] of kings" (*Inst.* 4.20.31; OS 5:501.17 and 23; translation modified). Here is a distinct echo of the curbing, punishing, inflicting recompense on, and taking up arms against tyrants that we found with the divinely appointed agents a little earlier. Now there is a slight difference: withstanding or intervening (the basic sense of *intercedere*) is slightly milder than curbing, punishing, and taking up arms, but the difference is not so great. Precisely what this withstanding or intervening may be is left unstated, but it is perfectly clear that absolute monarchs have no place in Calvin's polity. Nor indeed do kings who get too full of themselves and act in a tyrannical or licentious fashion.

We seem to have an answer to our problem of what to do with ungodly rulers. If you are a member of the common people, all you can do is obey and bear an ungodly ruler as best you can. But if you happen to be a magistrate, then you may do what is necessary to ensure that the king does the right thing by the people. And if you are a king, then you must put aside any pretension to absoluteness, for at the first sign of tyranny, God may crush you or a magistrate may oppose you. So we have two propositions: (1) the people must obey kings in all situations; and (2) God and/or the magistrate are to keep a check on rapacious kings. It seems as though we have a cautious formula for political stability. Indeed, Calvin seems to have laid down a polity with some decent checks and balances in place: a kingship kept in check by a magistrate, who I assume is appointed from within the aristocracy that Calvin so favors as the ruling body.

Calvin lays down this careful argument by section 31 of the last chapter of the *Institutes*. The problem is that it is the penultimate section. Calvin knows full well that there are some final biblical texts with which he has not dealt. And they will undo all the careful work he has invested in this long final chapter.

Let Princes Hear and Be Afraid

A little earlier I identified a move by Calvin that would have profound consequences for his argument. At the point where he specifies the two ways in which a ruler might be resisted and removed—by God directly or by a designated agent—he introduces the following principle: Because a ruler is subject to God, any ruler who does not obey and serve God will be dealt with severely. At that point he is careful to stipulate that only God or his agent may do the dirty work. But what happens when the people have to endure an ungodly or self-serving ruler? The answer with which we have become familiar is that the people should do nothing but endure. The last thing Calvin wants to do is give license to insurrection. So we find him asserting the following:

> But however these deeds of men are judged in themselves, still the Lord accomplished his work through them alike when *he broke the bloody scepters of arrogant kings and when he overturned intolerable governments. Let the princes hear and be afraid* [*Audiant principes, et tereantur*]. But we must, in the meantime, be very careful not to despise or violate that authority of magistrates, full of venerable majesty,

> which God has established by the weightiest of decrees, even though it may reside with the most unworthy of men, who defile it as much as they can with their own wickedness.
>
> (*Inst.* 4.20.31; *OS* 5:501.5–13; emphasis added)

This is a fascinating and highly revealing passage. The first point to make is that here the tension between the reactionary and the radical, between the conservative and revolutionary, shows up in all its glory. So, on the one hand, we find statements warning us not to violate the authority of magistrates, which is "full of venerable majesty," but then, on the other hand, we read of breaking "the bloody scepters of arrogant kings" and overthrowing "their intolerable governments." The text is almost at war with itself, moving one way and then the next. It is as though Calvin lets it rip only to hold himself back once again.

Further, I am particularly interested in the outburst against insolent and intolerable kings. For this passage is the second time Calvin has given vent to such political passion. We have already come across this slightly earlier one, but I cite it once again:

> *Before his face all kings shall fall and be crushed, and all the judges of the earth,* that have not kissed his anointed [Ps. 2:10-11], and all those who have written unjust laws to oppress the poor in judgment and to do violence to the cause of the lowly, to prey upon widows and rob the fatherless [Isa. 10:1-2].
>
> (*Inst.* 4.20.29; *OS* 5:500.8–13; emphasis added)

All kings and judges of the earth shall fall and be crushed; he will break the blood-soaked scepters of insolent kings and intolerable tyrants—a theme is certainly emerging here. What we have is nothing less than prophetic fury against oppressive and tyrannical rulers. However, up until this point Calvin must content himself with allowing God and his agents to do away with such tyrants. At least that is so until we come to that extraordinary final section of the last chapter of the *Institutes*.

SUBJECT ONLY IN THE LORD

I quote the passage again, this time with the Latin since I want to give it closer attention:

> But in that obedience which we have shown to be due the authority of rulers, we are always to make this exception, indeed, to observe it

as primary, that such obedience is never to lead us away from obedience to him, to whose will the desires of all kings ought to be subject, to whose decrees all their commands ought to yield, to whose majesty their scepters ought to be submitted. And how absurd would it be that in satisfying men you should incur the displeasure of him for whose sake you obey men themselves! The Lord, therefore, is the King of kings, who, when he has opened his sacred mouth, must alone be heard before all and above all men; next to him we are subject to those men who are in authority over us, but only in him. If they command anything against him, let it go unesteemed. And here let us not be concerned about all that dignity which the magistrates possess, for no harm is done to it when it is humbled before that singular and truly supreme power of God.

(*Inst.* 4.20.32)

At vero in ea, quam praefectorum imperiis deberi constituimus, obedientia, id semper excipiendum est, imo in primus observandum, ne ab eius obedientia nos deducat, cuius voluntati Regum omnium vota subesse, cuius decretis iussa cedere, cuius maiestati fasces submitti par est. Et vero, ut hominibus satisfacias, in eius offensionem incurrere, propter quem hominibus ipsis obedias, quam praeposterum fuerit? Dominus ergo Rex est regum: qui ubi sacrum os aperuit, unus pro omnibus simul ac supra omnes est audiendus; iis deinde qui nobis praesunt hominibus subiecti sumus: sed nonnisi in ipso. Adversus ipsum siquid imperent, nullo sit nec loco nec numero; neque hic totam illam, qua magistratus pollent, dignitatem quicquam moremur: cui iniuria nulla fit dum in ordinem, prae singulari illa vereque summa Dei potestate, cogitur.

(*OS* 5:501.28–502.3)

Finally the deeper impulse of Calvin's argument rises to the surface. He begins by recalling the obedience due the rulers, a point we can hardly forget given the way he has driven it home before. But then he introduces an "exception" (*excipiendum est*—literally, an exception must be made). Any obedience should not be incompatible with obedience to God. Or, as Calvin puts it in a finely balanced piece of writing, such obedience should never lead us away from obedience to the one to whom rulers are in fact subject (*ne ab eius obedientia nos deducat*). So we find three balanced subordinate clauses that follow this central statement, each of them introduced by "whose" (*cuius*): to whose will (*voluntati*), decrees (*decretis*), and majesty (*maiestati*) every king should be subject (*subesse*), must yield (*cedere*) and submit or bow (*submitti*). Each item—will, decree, majesty, being subject, yielding, and submitting—any garden-variety king would claim for himself. In response, Calvin points out that they all are in fact attributes of God first and kings second. He reinforces the point a sentence or two later, asserting that God is King of kings and that his is the mouth we should listen to "instead of all and above all" (*simul ac supra omnes*). Way back in that preface addressed to Francis, King of France—where Calvin is trying to assure the king that he means no seditious harm—we find exactly the same sentiment addressed directly to the king:

> Indeed, this consideration makes a true king: to recognize himself a minister of God in governing his kingdom. Now, that king who in ruling over his realm does not serve God's glory exercises not kingly rule but brigandage.
> (LCC 1:12; *OS* 3:11.29–32)[5]

Let the princes hear indeed! This quotation also suggests that the point Calvin makes at the end of the *Institutes* is not really an exception at all. If we go back to the opening sentence of the text I quoted above, we find that what Calvin has to say must be observed above everything else: *in primus observandum* (the gerund of *observo* giving the sense of obligation). Indeed, what Calvin writes here is hardly an exception at all but the basic rule for all engagements by Christians with the state.

The remainder of the quotation really turns around one point: when it comes to a choice between obeying God or obeying an ungodly ruler, there is no choice. The ruler loses out. Three times Calvin repeats what has become all too obvious. It would be simply "preposterous" (*praeposterum*) to suggest that anyone would attempt to please men and thereby incur the wrath of God. Then again, we may be subject to our rulers, as Calvin has asserted again and again, but "only in him" (*nonnisi in ipso*). And once again, as bluntly as possible, "If they command anything against him, let it be worth absolutely nothing" (*Adversus ipsum siquid imperent, nullo sit nec loco nec numero*). Or quite literally, "let it be from nothing, in no place and with no number." Nothing could clearer.

---

5. See also his closing comment to the exposition of the fifth commandment: "But we also ought in passing to note that we are bidden to obey our parents only 'in the Lord' [Eph. 6:1]. This is apparent from the principle already laid down. For they sit in that place to which they have been advanced by the Lord, who shares with them a part of his honor. Therefore, the submission paid to them ought to be a step toward honoring that highest Father. Hence, if they spur us to transgress the law, we have a perfect right to regard them not as parents, but as strangers who are trying to lead us away from obedience to our true Father. So should we act toward princes, lords, and every kind of superiors. It is unworthy and absurd for their eminence so to prevail as to pull down the loftiness of God. On the contrary, their eminence depends upon God's loftiness and ought to lead us to it" (*Inst.* 2.8.38; *OS* 3:379.16–27).

I cannot emphasize how much of a breakthrough these last lines are. This position may seem obvious now, but it was not so clear a little earlier where we were enjoined in no uncertain terms to obey even unjust, oppressive, and willful rulers for our own edification. I will return to this tension in a moment, but first an observation. When I first read this passage I assumed that Calvin was talking about magistrates. The word does appear towards the end, and I had been told that Calvin did not endorse civil disobedience by the people. Only the magistrate can curb, check, or even punish ungodly rulers. This would have the minimal benefit of maintaining some consistency within Calvin's own argument. The problem with such an argument is twofold. First, this passage from Calvin mentions kings (*Regum*) and rulers (*praefectorum*) along with magistrates. *All* rulers come under the same principle. And that is the second problem with the superficial consistency that might have been maintained. To do so would betray a far deeper theological truth for Calvin: God is supreme, and any obedience is due entirely to him. Rulers constitute no exception.

All too often we come across efforts to solve the contradictions in Calvin's thought. I prefer to take the other path and push these contradictions as far as they will go. And here we have a central contradiction: either obey the rulers at all costs, or obey God at all costs. Such a position works when there is no tension between the two, when the ruler's guidelines coincide with those of God. But when they clash, we have a problem. Calvin tries to mediate between the two, so he begins by arguing that the people should obey the rulers in all situations, even when they are rapacious, oppressive, and ungodly. Only God or his appointed avengers may punish such rulers, or indeed the magistrate, who is one such appointed agent.

But then Calvin realizes that there is more at stake, far more. It all turns on his theological position and his view of Scripture: if one's ultimate obedience is to God, there can be no compromise, and any ruler who decrees laws that contradict those of God must be shunned. Even more, all of us are radically fallen and depraved; that includes rulers as well. Thus, a ruler will more often than not tend to be oppressive and tyrannical, for he or she is a fallen creature like everyone else. I have indicated earlier the radically democratic nature of this position. Further, Calvin is far too good a student of the Bible to let his earlier position stand. What I mean here is that he knows all too well that we have stories of civil disobedience, refusal to obey unjust laws, and outright rebellion in the Bible. He cites texts such as Daniel's refusal to bow to

Nebuchadnezzar's decree to worship him (Dan. 6:22), or the edict of Peter in Acts 5:29 to obey God rather than men (see also Calvin 1844a, 214–15), or indeed Paul's comment on not yielding to the depraved wishes of men (1 Cor. 7:23). In fact, Calvin glosses this text from Paul as the last statement of the *Institutes*: "That we have been redeemed by Christ at so great a price as our redemption cost him, so that we should not enslave ourselves to the wicked desires of men—much less be subject to their impiety" [1 Cor. 7:23] (*Inst.* 4.20.32; *OS* 5:502.28–31). Or even more strongly in his commentary on Daniel 6:22, he writes,

> For earthly princes lay aside all their power when they rise up against God, and are unworthy of being reckoned in the number of mankind. We ought rather to utterly defy than to obey them whenever they are so restive and wish to spoil God of his rights, and, as it were, to seize upon his throne and draw him down from heaven.
> (Calvin 1852a, 382)

The outcome of Calvin's careful attention to the Bible is that he actually replicates the many-layered contradictions of that collection of texts. I will explore this point in more detail in the following chapter, but let me finish on a different point. The tension I have been tracing may also be cast in terms of compromise over against principle. For much of this last chapter of the *Institutes*, Calvin tries to find a compromise between obedience to rulers and obedience to God. We have seen the results of that compromise—the people must obey rulers at all costs: God and his agents may punish the rulers—but in the end it cannot hold. The principled Calvin triumphs in the end, and that principle is none other than obedience to God first and then his Scripture.

To my mind this is the mark of a true revolutionary: one who does not compromise the ideal and holds to it. It also has another unexpected revolutionary outcome. If God is in the business of punishing, avenging, curbing, and removing unjust and ungodly rulers, then God is the true revolutionary of Calvin's thought. It looks as though our revolutionary cat has been shown a wide-open mouth to the theological bag. This time Calvin is not going to clamp it shut.

6
Paul
Inheriting an Insight

Throughout this book I have traced a number of overlapping tensions in Calvin's thought—between the radical potential of a high view of the Bible and Calvin's reticence, between the radical breakthrough of grace and Calvin's attempts to channel it along acceptable lines, between Christian freedom and legalism, and between obedience to divinely appointed rulers and the obedience to God at the expense of any earthly rulers. All of these turn on a basic struggle within Calvin between his innate conservatism and his radical insights into theology and the Bible.

This chapter shifts gear, moving away from the close readings of select sections of the *Institutes* and daring a major hypothesis. The hypothesis is that Calvin inherited his tensions from the Bible for two reasons: first, he was too good a reader of the Bible not to pick them up; second, his situation at the crossroads between feudalism and capitalism is analogous to the tensions we find in the New Testament between clashing economic systems. Of course, this argument would require a book on its own to substantiate, so what I propose here is an incisive sketch, an effort to see the whole picture rather than getting lost in the detail. Many avoid such efforts like the plague, preferring as they do the endless qualifications and footnotes that turn off most readers.

INHERITING AN INSIGHT

I have come away from my intense engagement with Calvin with the distinct sense that he was far too good an exegete of the Bible not to notice, face, and try to deal with its myriad tensions and contradictions. This means that the simultaneously theological and political (or theologicopolitical) tension in Calvin's work is indebted to the Bible. I can well imagine Calvin insisting on lengthy Bible readings at the dinner table, with none of those present permitted to leave until the text had been read, commented on, and prayed over. So it was in my own family. No matter what the situation, whether sitting at the smallish dinner table at home, in an old canvas tent in the middle of the rain, or even around a campfire after the evening meal, my father would pull out a Bible, locate the bookmark from the previous evening, and continue on with the next chapter or three. Even if we fretted to continue whatever game we were playing at the time, it did ensure that, ever since, the biblical stories have always felt like second nature.

So I am seeking Calvin the careful Bible reader.[1] I am not, however, after the Calvin who seeks to reconcile and mediate contrary biblical positions (we have seen enough of that). Rather, I am interested in the way these contradictory elements of the Bible manifest themselves within Calvin's own text, and in how Calvin almost too faithfully replicates the tensions of the Bible in his own thought. After all, if you have as high a view of Scripture as Calvin did, then it is difficult to avoid incarnating these biblical tensions in your own thought.

Reading a Multivocal Text Univocally

Let me put it this way: Calvin tried to read the Bible univocally but ended up reading it multivocally. Here we have the crux of a massive and continuing debate: on the one side, there is the long tradition of theological and ecclesial interpreters of the Bible who maintain that it is ultimately a univocal text. Those originally responsible for the canon thought they had managed to put together a univocal collection. Ever since, there has been a consistent assumption and effort to show that the Bible speaks with one voice. After all, if you believe that God is one, that he is omniscient, omnipotent, and (above all) consistent, then you

---

1. For a good recent survey of Calvin's exegetical strategies, see the collection edited by McKim (2006).

will want the text of his revelation to be equally consistent. One God speaks with one voice in one Bible.

On the other side there is an equally long tradition that accords pride of place to the multivocal nature of the Bible. It is not some postmodern invention that overrides a much older tradition; no, it goes back to the very nature of the text itself. As I have argued elsewhere (Boer 2007c, 56–66), the process of canonization was a desperate effort to control an unruly and fractious collection of texts, a collection that is by no means happy with being contained in such a way. As a quick comparison, what would a collection of major English texts gathered over the last millennium look like? At the least, we would need to include Chaucer's *Canterbury Tales*, Shakespeare's plays, James Joyce's *Ulysses*, the Magna Carta, the American Declaration of Independence, the English translation of *The Manifesto of the Communist Party*, and so on. It would be exceedingly difficult to avoid the conclusion that such a collection of key texts from the last millennium has a range of political, let alone theological, positions: so also with the Bible. I find that Ernst Bloch expresses the multivocality of the Bible best: it may often be "a scandal to the poor and not always a folly to the rich," but it is also "the Church's bad conscience" (Bloch 1972, 25 and 21). Both are true: the Bible has often been taken as a friend of the wealthy ruling class, *and* it has been an inspiration for revolutionary groups seeking to overthrow their rich and powerful oppressors.

Now, I hardly need to argue at length for the multivocal and multivalent nature of the Bible, but what interests me is the way such multivocality is the raison d'être of biblical criticism (see further Boer forthcoming a). Take the allegorical interpretation of the Bible that held sway for a millennium and a half: the very possibility of interpretation depends on some anomaly or contradiction that then becomes the trigger for multiple levels of interpretation. And these levels, restricted to four to curtail the greater flights of interpretive fancy, were themselves a recognition of the many voices of the Bible. Or take the historical criticism that succeeded allegorical exegesis: now the bumps and contradictions of the text become the basis for theories of sources or oral traditions, all of which then needs a theory to account for how they came to be the texts we know.

What we find then is not that the Bible is either univocal or multivocal, but that both features are at war with each other. For a while now I have been engaged in a debate with George Aichele over this matter (Aichele 2001; Boer 2007c). Aichele sees the act of canonization as the determining feature of the very idea of a Bible: it was created as a unitary and univocal text. Only after this fact, argues Aichele, does multivocality arise in tension with the primary univocality. My own preference is to see the many voices of the Bible as the initial problem with which canonization and biblical interpretation then have to struggle.

But it is a debate that shares much common ground. Its relevance for my discussion of Calvin is that he consciously thought he was interpreting the Bible in a univocal fashion (it did after all come from the mouth of God), but his careful attention to the Bible led him unconsciously to a multivocal reading. Let me spin this out. Calvin tries to read the Bible as a univocal text revealed by one God: one text, one God.[2] So we find him twisting and weaving his way between very different texts in order to produce a seemingly coherent and logical argument that links them all together.[3] Of course, this univocal text from the one God is the one that agrees all too well with Calvin's own position.

However, as we have seen time and again, Calvin's high view of Scripture and his careful attention to the text led him in a very different direction—towards a multivocal reading despite himself. Let us see how he gets there. To begin with, he is too faithful a reader of the Bible to dismiss and avoid texts that cause him problems, to find a convenient collection known in the trade as a "canon within the canon" that suits his position. Like few others, he reads *all* the relevant texts (he did after all write commentaries on almost all the Bible).[4] Most of the time he is able to give the impression that he has a robust, logical, and coherent argument that makes sense of these very different and often contradictory texts. Often he pulls it off, but equally as often he does not. His arguments can be coherent and logical in appearance, but in reality they are not. Or as I prefer to put it, in their twists and turns his arguments actually embody the contradictions he tries to resolve. This is what I mean by suggesting that Calvin reveals the multivocality of the Bible unconsciously: he does it despite his best intentions. And at odd moments there is an astonishing recognition of such multivocality. For example, in commenting on 1 Corinthians 6:16, he writes, "If, however, any one does not altogether approve of this exposition, as being rather forced, I shall bring forward another" (Calvin 1848, 218). On the surface it seems as though he is being modest, recognizing that his first offering is not as

---

2. See the long chapter on the doctrine of God (*Inst.* 1.13; *OS* 3:108-51); see also J. Thompson (2004).

3. Some of the best examples are when he has to deal with the large number of biblical texts that clearly assume a doctrine of retribution/reward for one's acts (*Inst.* 3.16; *OS* 4:248-53) and when he sets out to explain an equally large number of biblical texts where free will turns up (*Inst.* 2.5.6; *OS* 3:303.27–304.30).

4. Calvin wrote commentaries on all books except Ruth, Esther, Song of Solomon, Ecclesiastes, Job, Proverbs, and Revelation.

persuasive as it might be and then offering a second interpretation that comes a little closer to the one truth. But the very fact that Calvin offers another interpretation means that he also recognizes, in spite of himself, that there is more than one way to read a text, that it may have multiple meanings. This is the Calvin that interests me, the one who inherits the political ambivalence if not multivalency of the Bible in the intensity of his reading practice and the complexity of his arguments.

Paul's Ambivalence

At this point I would like to focus on Paul, especially because Calvin was heavily indebted to Paul for his key positions.[5] What is intriguing about Paul is that he struggles with a series of conflicts and oppositions. They keep turning up: Jews and Gentiles (Rom. 2:8–10; 3:9, 29; 9:24; 10:12; 1 Cor. 1:23; Gal. 2), slave and free (Rom. 6; 1 Cor. 7:20–22; 12:13; Gal. 3:28), male and female (Gal. 3:28), flesh and spirit (Rom. 7; 1 Cor. 6:16; 15:39, 50; Gal. 6:13; Phil. 3:1–4), elect and damned (Rom. 9:11; 11:7, 28), Adam and Christ (Rom. 5:11–13, 16–18; 1 Cor. 15:22), death and life (Rom. 5–6; 7:10; 8:2, 6, 38; 2 Cor. 2:16; 2 Cor. 4:10–12; Phil. 1:20), grace and law (Rom. 4:16; 5:20; 6:14–15; Gal. 2:21; 3:18; 5:4), grace and sin (Rom. 5:20–21; 6:1, 14–15), grace and works (Rom. 11:6), Christ and law (Rom. 7:4, 25; 8:2; 10:4; 1 Cor. 9:21; Gal. 2:16, 21; 3:1, 13, 24; 5:4; 6:2; Phil. 3:9), Christ and sin (Rom. 5:21; 6:1, 9–11, 23; 7:25; 8:2, 9–10; 13:14; 1 Cor. 8:12; 15:3, 17; 2 Cor. 5:19; Gal. 2:17; 3:22; 5:14), righteousness through faith or works (Rom. 1:17; 3:21–22; 4:1–25; 9:13; 10:6; Gal. 3:11; 5:5; Phil. 3:9), law of sin and law of Christ (Rom. 7:25; 8:2). I have given a rather comprehensive list to emphasize just how consistent these oppositions are.

Now, Paul tackles these oppositions in different ways. Sometimes one side receives his approving nod, and the other side does not (it is not too difficult to sort these out). At other times he mixes and matches: Christ and grace are pivots for many of the terms Paul values, so we can line up Christ and/or grace with redemption, life, and faith and oppose them to sin, law, death, works, and so on.[6] And at other

---

5. I must admit that I am not a great fan of Paul. Although I have written on Paul (Boer 2006; 2007e; 2007b, 335–90; 2008; 2007a), I still find that when I read his letters my mind wanders, and before I know it, I am nodding off, the Bible slipping from my grasp and waking me with a thump on the floor.

6. At this point we could extend this mixing in a way that would reveal some of Paul's more problematic assumptions. For example, what do the reshuffled oppositions of elect versus female, or law versus spirit, or indeed Jews versus life, say about Paul's own deeper patterns of thought?

times he mentions an opposition in order to point out that it no longer applies in light of Christ (the famous male and female, slave and free, Jew and Gentile of Gal. 3:28). At yet others, the opposition becomes the basis of further complication, undermining, and rearranging, such as the reshaping of law versus grace in terms of the law of Christ versus the law of sin, or the jumbling of flesh and spirit in light of the body and in terms of death and life.

Two features of these differing contradictions are of use to my argument. First, the famous opposition of law and grace—usually coupled with faith and works—was one that Calvin and the other Reformers took as a slogan. What is curious about this opposition is how it works itself out in Paul's (rather meager) collection of texts. While Paul asserted freedom from the law because of grace, some of the early churches took the idea much further than he anticipated, pushing Christian freedom from the law into all manner of directions, such as freedom in regard to sex, worship, Roman law, and so on. As some of the classic studies of the Corinthian and Galatian correspondence have argued, Paul seems to be putting out fires for which he himself was initially responsible.[7] While the Galatians erred on the side of sticking with the law, the Corinthians pursued Paul's arguments much further than he was willing to countenance. So we find the classic libertine response: if the law has been overcome, then it is no longer relevant for us. Alternatively, if our sins have been forgiven once and for all, then it matters not what we do. Or in an apocalyptic vein: since Christ has inaugurated the last days, the old world has passed and has no hold on us now.

Once these various readings became clear to Paul, he realized with some shock what he had let loose. The push towards Christian freedom that appears in the Letter to the Galatians runs into the mud in the Corinthian correspondence. To his own chagrin, these developments could claim a logical beginning within his own thought. So we find him trying to rope in what has taken off, setting boundaries on what grace, faith, and freedom mean—not to dispense with the law entirely, for it is good, arguing that there is another law, the law of Christ, banning the sexual license that some saw in the idea, limiting the freedom that women were taking in some of the churches, urging some concern for "weaker" believers in outward observance (meat given to idols and so on). So we find that

---

7. See Longenecker (1990), Martyn (2004), Matera (2007), Martin (1999), Thistleton (2000), Keener (2005), and Fitzmyer (2008). For the sake of argument, I assume with the bulk of studies of Paul that his references to opponents and opposing positions actually reflect real opponents. It would be far more interesting (but a different study) to explore the possibility that Paul manufactures these opponents in a deft piece of rhetorical shadowboxing. By doing so, he brings his readers onside by arraying himself against a range of imaginary opponents.

the same person who wrote "not under the law, but under grace" (Rom. 6:14–15) and "Now we are discharged from the law, dead to that which held us captive" (Rom. 7:6) also wrote, "Let every person be subject to the governing authorities.... Whoever resists authority resists what God has appointed" (Rom. 13:1). The same mouth that dictated "All who rely on works of the law are under a curse" (Gal. 3:10) also mentions that "we uphold the law" (Rom. 3:31), that the law is "holy" and "good" (Rom. 7:11 and 16). One more: to the Galatians Paul writes, "There is neither slave nor free; . . . for you are all one in Christ Jesus" (Gal. 3:28 RSV), while he tells the Corinthians, "Every one should remain in the state in which he was called" (1 Cor. 7:20 RSV).

Calvin Reading Paul

What does Calvin make of these tensions within Paul's texts? He often felt that he was back in the time of the apostles, or at least that their times were very similar to his own. So, in that famous letter to the king of France he points out that the apostles too struggled with antinomians. He cites Romans 6:1, 15 to show that Paul too struggled with wayward interpretations of his own texts: "They were despisers of God who, when they heard that sin abounded that grace might more abound, immediately concluded, 'We shall remain in sin, that grace may abound' [cf. Rom. 6:1]. When they heard that believers were not under the law, straightway they chirped: 'We shall remain in sin because we are not under the law, but under grace' [cf. Rom. 6:15]" (LCC 1:29; OS 3:28.2-7; see also *Inst.* 3.20.45; OS 4:360.14–18). Calvin calls them unstable and unlearned false prophets, who led people to destruction. We don't have to scratch too far to see the Münster Revolution behind this text. A similar sense pervades the commentary on the Corinthian epistles (1848), where Calvin finds Paul combating many of the "excesses" that Calvin found all too pervasive in his own day. By contrast, the criticisms of external observance of the law in Galatians remind Calvin again and again of the Roman Church (1854b). Caught between the legalizing and ceremonial stress of Rome (Galatians) and the libertine directions of the Anabaptists (Corinth), Calvin seems to have been perfectly, if somewhat uncomfortably, at home. But note also that Calvin draws inspiration from the apostles: just as they stepped out boldly in the face of peril and scandal in order to proclaim the truth, so also should he and others like him do the same.

What I would like to do for a few moments is see what Calvin made of these tensions in his central commentary on Romans, as well as those on Galatians and 1 Corinthians.[8] No prizes for guessing what he identifies as the central theme of the whole Epistle to the Romans—justification by faith. But then it gets interesting. Soon enough, Calvin points out that Paul operates by the "comparing of contraries" (Calvin 1844b, xxvi), and so he follows suit. The first great opposition is a winner-take-all: the righteousness of works versus justification by faith, or as he puts it in the commentary on Galatians, the works of the law versus justification by free grace (Calvin 1854b, 18). One must vanish in place of the other. Soon enough we find others that fall into the same pattern: grace, righteousness, gospel, and faith all line up against sin, carnal lusts, impiety, profanation, vanity, judgment, condemnation, and even "the horrible sin of preposterous lust" (Calvin 1844b, 33)—or to sum it all up, destruction versus salvation. In the case of these oppositions, one must step aside, and the other must take its place.

But then another opposition emerges, that between Jew and Gentile (or "Greek," as he more properly calls them in the commentary), and here Calvin takes a different track, especially when commenting on Romans 2:11–29; Romans 9–11; as well as Galatians 2:11–16. Both Jew and Gentile are unceremoniously lumped together; both sides of this divide are guilty of outward holiness and inward wickedness. And both certainly are in need of salvation. The radically democratic drive of utter depravity turns up here, for even though Paul deals with them one at a time (the Gentiles are convicted through their conscience, but the Jews, through the law), they are both equally condemned and equally in need of redemption. No one can claim any privilege due to some covenant, virtue, or election; they cannot "hem in the grace of God" (Calvin 1844b, xxv) in some fashion; and they cannot, as the Gentiles do, plead ignorance because they had not heard of God's law. However, the stark difference with the first opposition is that the Jew-Gentile distinction is one to be overcome. In this case, you do not take sides; you make a dialectical leap beyond it.

What happens is that everyone must pass through judgment and condemnation in order to come face-to-face with justification by faith:

> Thus, when he hath deprived all mankind, both of the truth of their own virtue, and also of the glory of righteousness, and thrown them

---

8. The following is drawn from Calvin's Romans commentary (1844b), as well as those on Galatians (1854b) and 1 Corinthians (1848; 1849c).

down with the severity of God's judgment, he cometh unto that which he purposed; namely, that we are justified by faith, showing what faith that is, and how we obtain thereby the righteousness of God.

(Calvin 1844b, xxv; see also 25)

What we really have here is a passage from one point to another, from judgment to justification, from condemnation to redemption. And it is a passage for all humanity—which is really what the code of Jew and Gentile means for Calvin.

Once we have Jew and Gentile, we can't avoid the other pairs from Galatians 3:28—male and female, and slave and free. Calvin's comment on this text is surprisingly brief:

> The meaning is, that there is no distinction of persons here, and therefore it is of no consequence to what nation or condition any one may belong: nor is circumcision any more regarded than sex or civil rank. And why? Because Christ makes us all one. Whatever may have been their former differences, Christ alone is able to unite them all.
>
> (Calvin 1854b, 112)

It looks like the democracy of depravity has passed over into the democracy of salvation—it makes no difference to what sex or class or even ethnic group one belongs, for Christ "makes us all one." I suspect that this text did not impress Calvin, for he passes by it too quickly. By contrast, in his comments on 1 Corinthians 7:20–22, Calvin (1848, 248–50) stresses the Paul who counsels slaves to remain content with their station in life. Indeed, the impression of a democratic salvation soon passes, for Calvin reserves texts such as these only for the elect. Only insofar as the Jews and Gentiles, men and women, and slaves and free are of the elect will they become one in Christ, in which no privilege or status counts. In other words, the democracy of depravity becomes the aristocracy of salvation. More of that later.

Thus far, Calvin has dealt with the Pauline oppositions in two ways: he clearly takes sides with one pole of the opposition, or rather he advocates a passage from the undesirable side to the more desirable one, and then he argues for the overcoming of other oppositions such as Jew and Gentile by means of this passage. When he gets to Romans 7 (see also Gal. 2), a third approach turns up: the negative side is transformed. In that great discussion of law, sin, life, death, spirit, and flesh, Calvin focuses on the law. Struck by the way Paul calls the law good and holy, Calvin points out that Paul clears the law from all reproach (Calvin 1844b, 179–80). It is not the law's fault if it could not save and if its only effect was condemnation; that is our fault, for we through sin have turned the law into an agent of death. Here we find the basis of the redemption of the law in Calvin's theology: now it becomes a sure guide for the sanctified life, or the law of the spirit of life (Rom. 8:2; see Calvin 1844, 194–95). As is well known, he picks up Paul's cue in Romans 4 (Abraham's justification by faith) and argues for the priority of justification by faith over justification by the law. That move allows him to place grace first and the law second; or, to give justification priority and sanctification a runner-up position. So the law has been transformed and redeemed, but what of the other oppositions that turn up in relation to it? This is where some of those oppositions that initially looked like we had to dump the negative and pick up the positive begin to change. For example, in the contrary of Adam and Christ, it is no longer a case of dropping Adam for Christ but of transforming him in light of Christ. Even works undergo a transformation: though not even the works that God does through us can gain us righteousness (Calvin 1844b, 80), there are works that one does as part of the sanctification after one has been redeemed and justified. Like the law, these works are acceptable as long as they show one's gratitude and not one's pride. Unfortunately, flesh and Spirit do not fare so well in Calvin's exegesis. There is no transformation of flesh as we found with law, works, and death. Calvin is far too Augustinian to give the flesh and its concupiscence much space: the children of God are shut within the prison of this mortal body, and the Spirit struggles against the threat of the flesh.

However, death fares somewhat better. Initially, death is the way the law bends because of our own sin, and death joins all the others—sin, flesh, licentious liberty, judgment, and condemnation. But then we find a crucial shift, for death is itself transformed in the resurrection of Christ. At this point we come upon the key to Calvin's reading of Paul. The death and resurrection of Christ provides the base narrative for all of the other oppositions.[9] This is the passage from one side to the other that I mentioned earlier, the transition from one pole to another. The catch is that the oppositions are affected differently by this narrative of passage. In some cases the negative term is left behind: sin,

---

9. As he puts it in the *Institutes*: "Therefore we divide the substance of our salvation between Christ's death and resurrection as follows: through his death, sin was wiped out and death extinguished; through his resurrection, righteousness was restored and life raised up, so that—thanks to his resurrection—his death manifested its power and efficacy in us" (*Inst.* 2.16.13; *OS* 3:500.12–16).

righteousness by works, the law of sin and death, condemnation, flesh, impiety, and carnal lusts are all dropped by the roadside on the way to redemption, while grace, justification by faith, Spirit, the law of life and Christ, and justification take their place. In other cases the negative is transformed in the process: so we find the law redeemed through grace for the sake of sanctification, or death transformed into life, and Adam renovated by Christ. And in other cases, the opposition itself makes the transition from death to resurrection: this is especially true of Jew and Gentile, but also of male and female, and slave and free.

In this last case there is one caveat: not all make the passage successfully. Jew and Gentile may be united in the democracy of depravity, but when we pass to redemption, a new distinction appears, namely, that between the elect and the damned. The key verses of Romans 8:29–30 (Calvin 1844b, 225–30) play a massive role for this distinction, one that became crucial in Calvin's whole system. While the former are "freed from the danger and fear of condemnation," the latter are "not partakers of this so great benefit" (Calvin 1844b, xxviii). From this point on, the lines are clearly drawn, and Calvin can take all of Paul's comments concerning sanctification as relevant only to the elect. So we have come back to our first group of oppositions, those of sin and grace, Spirit and flesh, works and faith. While the reprobate are unloaded along with these undesirables, the elect link arms with all the positive, transformed, and overcome terms of Calvin's analysis of Paul. Or rather, they are the beneficiaries of the law, Adam, and death itself transformed through spirit, faith, and above all, grace.

What are we to make of these different ways of negotiating the Pauline oppositions? Calvin has his own preferences. For example, he plays up the matter of election, so much so that he reserves what seem to be the more universalizing statements of Paul for those predestined to salvation. Even within that small group, Calvin is rather lukewarm when it comes to the abolition of differences between Jew and Gentile, male and female, or slave and free. But he does draw out the complex and tricky oppositions between law and grace, and death and life.

Thus far I have argued that Calvin is too faithful a reader of Paul to miss the complexities of these oppositions. However, I am hardly one to argue that he has actually figured Paul out or that he is the true interpreter of Paul to the exclusion of all others. That he tended to think he was or that plenty of Reformers would agree that he was makes no difference whatsoever. What I do want to argue is that he was a very good and persuasive interpreter of Paul, so much so that he replicates Paul's own tensions and confusions. It is surely an argument with a twist: Calvin is an excellent interpreter of a man who was not always too clear himself. Calvin is not the only one who is a good interpreter of Paul, nor is he the only one to offer an intriguing and persuasive interpretation, for there is (to state the blindingly obvious) no one true interpretation.

CALVIN AND PAUL IN CONTEXT

There is another level to my argument, one that relies on context. One of the major reasons that Calvin produced such a powerful and epoch-making interpretation of Paul is that their contexts are analogous. Starkly put, in the same way that Calvin sought to negotiate at an ideological level the massive changes under way in the slow transition from feudalism to capitalism, so also does Paul navigate, again ideologically, the difficult passage from one socioeconomic system to another. Let me dig this proposition out a little.

A basic assumption of this argument is that the realms of thought, theology, and writing are not divorced from their historical context. These activities do not take place in an autonomous capsule; rather, they are bound by intricate webs to that context. Not many would argue against such an assumption, but the question then concerns the nature of those connections. A common track for many commentators is to explore the day-to-day or chronicle-like events in which Calvin lived and worked. For example, I have exploited the following in my argument: Calvin had to find a path between the periodic explosions of anarchist politics and the wary reaction of princes and kings, between the simmering criticism of the Anabaptists and the rearguard actions of the Roman Catholics. This is fine as far it goes, but it really doesn't get down to the deeper issues at stake in Calvin's work. For those we need to consider socioeconomic formations, or what are sometimes called modes of production. At this point I need to plow through a little theory.

The persuasive and very useful position I follow may be described as "imaginary resolution," or more fully as an "imaginary resolution of a real contradiction." It has a rich pedigree, running from Claude Lévi-Strauss (1989, 229–56) through Louis Althusser (1971, 127–86), Fredric Jameson (1981, 77–80), and Michael Sprinker (1987) into our own day. Let me explain: Such a theory begins by noting that the search for an author's intention is a distraction, albeit one that continues to bedevil much interpretation, especially in biblical and theological research. Intention does count, but it is a minor element among many others. What this theory foregrounds is the role of unconscious forces, or in Freudian terms the far more powerful subconscious elements of our thought and lives. The core of the theory is that difficult and irresolvable social tensions will show up in the cultural products of a society, whether that is literature, art, film, television, or what have you. Those cultural products will attempt to resolve the tensions in many possible fashions. Some may offer an alternative reality (as we find in science fiction or utopian works); others may present a story that violently breaks through the tensions (as in many works that solve the story's problems through a violent conflagration at the end); and others may do so through formal innovation (new genres in the mixture of old ones, new styles of painting, and so on).

As an example, let me turn to none other than Claude Lévi-Strauss. In *Tristes tropiques* (1989, 229–56), which is one of the best books I have ever read, he offers a reading of facial art among different indigenous tribes in South America. His interest was drawn to the facial decorations of the tribes he visited, especially the Caduveo. But those decorations indicate a tension, argues Lévi-Strauss, for they are based on an axis at an oblique angle to the face. That is, rather than use the natural lines of nose, mouth, and eyes, the Caduveo patterns follow another axis at an angle to these natural lines. Lévi-Strauss suggests that the reason for two axes in these face decorations is that, unlike the neighboring Guana and Bororo, who have the social checks and balances of moieties to mitigate their caste system, the Caduveo have no such social solution. Their art becomes another means of dealing with social tensions. In other words, they made use of facial decoration to ameliorate and repress the social tensions between social groups within the tribe. The catch is that in the very effort to deal with such a tension, the art reveals it at a formal level.

So also with Calvin's theology and biblical exegesis: they function as a persuasive imaginary resolution of the seismic shifts taking place in social and economic terms. And that shift was the rocky breakup of feudal social and economic relations and the explosions and ruptures of the newer capitalist ones. This long revolution, with high points such as the Enlightenment and Reformation and low points such as the enclosure movements (especially in Britain) and the Peasants' Wars in Germany, has been mapped, perused, and analyzed by a long string of scholars. As one or two examples among many, Michael Perelman (2000) uncovers the way capitalist social relations—with the wage relationship, the selling of labor power by workers to employers, and the need to adapt bodies and daily rhythms to that of the industrial process—had to be enforced at the point of a sword or at the end of a gun. These patterns and assumptions of life are hardly "normal" for those used to the very different cycles of feudal production, so people had to be wrenched, often with much suffering, into the new system. Or as E. P. Thompson (1966) has traced for a later period (seventeenth- and eighteenth-century England), the establishment of England as the preeminent industrial and colonial power required the creation, extreme brutalization, and then self-conscious resistance of that new class known as the working class (see also Engels 1975).

Calvin provides a highly successful theological narrative that enabled people to cope with such a transition. It is a classic imaginary resolution of a deep social contradiction, namely, that between feudalism and capitalism. Calvin was an instrumental figure in both mapping that change and enabling people to deal with it. What I mean here is that the narrative of a passage from death to life, from law to grace, from flesh to spirit, from outer observance to inner compulsion, is a narrative that enables people to come to terms with the changes taking place in their own social and economic situation. While that situation may be too large or complex to understand, the story of the death and resurrection of the Christ enables them to put such a situation into a recognizable narrative form. The old system, embodied by the Church of the time, of justification by works must give way to a new system of justification by faith. Some elements will not make the passage, such as sin or flesh, but others will pass over to be transformed, especially the law, works, and death itself. Indeed, death and resurrection are extraordinarily powerful metaphors for such a seismic shift in economic relations.

Now, lest I be accused of reducing it all to the "ultimately determining instance" of the economic, I suggest instead that my argument widens the power and influence of Calvin's theology. That theology has economic and social ramifications that are integral to his thought and cannot be placed in little boxes in the back of Calvin studies with labels such as "Calvin's social thought" or "Calvin's economics." But it may also encompass Max Weber's argument that Calvinist thought laid the groundwork for capitalist social relations and assumptions. My argument is more comprehensive than Weber's, for Calvin was not merely a lever or mediator for capitalist ideology; rather, he was one of the great symbolic theorists of the transition, and he provided a story to live by in such a transition.

I did promise another dimension to this argument, namely, that Calvin's relation to his context is analogous to that of Paul.[10] In other words, the contradictions that show up in Paul's texts are also creative and tension-ridden responses to socioeconomic tension and tumult. The various contradictions—grace and law, faith and works, Jew and Gentile, death and resurrection, and so on—may be seen as perpetual efforts at an intellectual and religious level to resolve a contradiction at a socioeconomic level, especially between clashing socioeconomic systems. As New Testament scholars with an economic ear (all too rare among such scholars) have shown, Palestine at the time struggled with the imposition of a slave-based system over the top of a far older economic system that had been the status quo in the ancient Near East for centuries.

Richard Horsley (1997) and those who follow him have been instrumental in highlighting the extraordinary transformations brought about in the Roman Empire by Augustus Caesar: the full-fledged development of the cult and gospel of the emperor, the centralization of patron-client relations in the emperor, and the profound impacts of such changes in regional cities such as Ephesus and Corinth. Above all, the infamous pax Romana turns out to be system of violence, blood, systematic destruction, and enslavement in order to expand and maintain the empire. Let me quote Horsley:

> During the first century B.C.E. Roman warlords took over the eastern Mediterranean, including Judea, where Pompey's troops defiled the Jerusalem Temple in retaliation for the resistance of the priests. The massive acts of periodic reconquest of the rebellious Judean and Galilean people included *thousands enslaved* at Magdala/Tarichaea in Galilee in 52–51 B.C.E., *mass enslavement* in and around Sepphoris (near Nazareth) and thousands crucified at Emmaus in Judea in 4

---

10. Here for once I give into the overwhelming drive to use context as the key to understanding Paul. Context seems to be the key, which is really another way of saying that history remains the sine qua non of Pauline studies. And that means going back and sorting out what Paul "really" meant in his first-century context. What one needs to do is locate an as-yet-neglected feature of this context, a feature that then becomes the secret passage to a new understanding of Paul. Out of the overlays and internal debates between the "old perspective" with its introspective and theological Paul (loosely everything before 1980), the old "new perspective" in which Paul must be understood in his Jewish context, and then the new "new perspective" where the Roman Empire becomes the key, we find study after study doing the same thing and returning to Paul's context. For example, we find the ideological place of the androgyne as the answer to the tension between universalism and dualism in Paul's writings (Boyarin 1994; 2004); or the Stoics who provide the inescapable philosophical and social background for Paul's thought (Swancutt 2004), so much so that he is a philosopher first (Engberg-Pedersen 2000); or the various *encomia, progymnasmata, physiognomics,* and other rhetorical treatises that provide us with a picture of collective "Mediterranean" notions of personality that must not be confused with "Western" individualist notions in our understanding of Paul (Malina and Neyrey 1996); or inheritance rights throughout the ancient Near East, Greece, and Rome, which give some sense to Paul's theme of adoption (Corley 2004); or Hellenistic perceptions of sexuality and the body that become the necessary background for reading Paul (Martin 1995); or the *psychagogia*, the "leading of souls" that runs through the moral philosophy of Greece and Rome, which gives us a sense of what Paul is about in Philippians (Smith 2005).

B.C.E., and the systematic devastation of villages and towns, destruction of Jerusalem and the Temple, and *mass enslavement* in 67–70 C.E. In the area of Paul's mission, the Romans ruthlessly sacked and torched Corinth, one of the most illustrious Greek cities, slaughtered its men, and *enslaved* its women and children in 146 B.C.E.

(Horsley 1997, 10–11; emphasis added)

I have not emphasized parts of this text for nothing, for mass enslavement is the key economic issue here. The Greeks and especially the Romans brought a new economic system to their empire, a slave-based system in which the slaves generated the necessary surplus so that the relatively few ruling and propertied "citizens" did not need so to work.[11] In economic terms, the extraction of surplus—what the slaves produced above their needs for subsistence—was extracted from them by those who owned them, thereby generating and maintaining their positions of wealth and power (see further Anderson 1974, 13–103). This slave-based system brutally and systematically replaced what I have elsewhere termed a Sacred Economy (Boer 2007d). It is, to use the terms of economic history, a violent shift from one mode of production to another, one that gradually transformed the Roman Empire. The imposition of a different economic and social system took place in a piecemeal fashion through systematic violence and disruption, especially in the three or four centuries at the turn of the era.

One of the most obvious signs of this shift in social formations is a high level of violence, social unrest, and conflict as the new system imposes itself on an older established one. Such troubled transitions produce displacement, tension, and violence in demographic, economic, social, political, and psychological terms. The quotation from Horsley brings this out all too clearly: revolt after revolt cruelly crushed, until the Romans became sufficiently sick and tired of it so as to destroy the temple in Jerusalem and ban Jews from entering the new city of Aelia Capitolina. One would have had to be a hermit from the moment of birth to avoid such seismic shifts, to steer clear of any political opinion whatsoever, or not to want to resolve such tensions and conflicts in some fashion or other. Paul, I would suggest, is no exception.

So the oppositions I have traced all too briefly in Paul's texts may be regarded as the manifestations of such a massive and brutal transition. One after another they roll out of his texts, only to be treated in

---

11. See both Sheila Briggs (2000) and the excellent book by Jennifer Glancy (2006), although a more systematic economic treatment would have strengthened these studies.

the various ways I suggested earlier. Each one is an alternative effort to deal with the fundamental socioeconomic tension. For instance, siding with one side of the equation becomes an ethical decision for one instead of the other—life over death, grace over law, faith over works. This taking of sides is really the first option open to someone faced with a crushing opposition. But then Paul also suggests that "in Christ" some of these oppositions are overcome. Here we have the famous trio of slave and free, Jew and Gentile, male and female. In this step, Paul makes a first effort at what we might call mediating the oppositions. One negates them by positing a greater and higher reality into which they are absorbed. A third option goes even further: in this case, Paul narrates a passage from one to the other, from death to life, from law to grace, from works to faith, and from sin to redemption. In the process, the first term is appropriated and transformed: so death becomes part of resurrection; law is still needed within grace; and works are transformed in faith. The connection with Calvin should be rather clear by now. Even more, the effort to resolve these contradictions in some way ensures that the contradictions remain crucial elements of his texts. And in this respect they are the strongest traces of Paul's troubled and ruptured socioeconomic context.

The risk of such a strategy is high. On the one hand, a transformative story like the death and resurrection of Jesus Christ—the key narrative that holds all the oppositions together—may offer a radical breakthrough. It seems as though some of those who first heard and read Paul, and then later Calvin, caught a glimpse of that breakthrough and wanted to take it further. With sin, law, works, as well as gender, ethnic, and economic divisions overcome by the story of Christ's death and resurrection, the possibility opened up for a very new world that might be realized here and now—sexually, communally, politically, economically. On the other hand, the way Paul replicates the socioeconomic tensions in the structure of his arguments, especially in terms of the oppositions I have been tracing, means that they may come back with a vengeance. Add to that the sense one sometimes gets that Paul himself was genuinely troubled by the radical possibilities of his thought, and we have a real tendency towards reaction. So a transformed law may end up being a far more totalitarian law than the previous one, or reformed works may become an obsession with a whole new set of works, or proclaiming the end of gender, ethnic, and economic tensions may avoid their very real presence in everyday life. Calvin was to take this reactionary possibility much further.

Paul, like Calvin, is deeply ambivalent. Consciously, he tries to tone down the more radical effects of his thought, a move that exacerbates the tensions. Unconsciously, he offers the possibility of a transformative breakthrough: the transformation and overcoming of the oppositions in his thought, all of them linked to the story of the death and resurrection of Christ, open up radical possibilities. Yet these same tensions are far too closely tied to the socioeconomic tensions of his context—between an older and highly resistant system (Sacred Economy) and the brutal new system based on slavery—so much so that the old realities of law, works, gender, ethnicity, and economy come back with a vengeance.

I close with a small example: the attitude to Empire (usually written without the "Roman"). An increasingly voluminous literature has been trying to argue that Paul and indeed the whole New Testament offers resistance to the Roman Empire. Apart from my misgivings at such an effort to detoxify and rescue the text once more (a deeply confessional effort), it simply does not measure up (see Moore 2006). Simply put, Paul is two-faced. He does at times seem to offer an alternative structure to those offered by the Roman Empire. It is an alternative "gospel"—not one of the emperor but of Jesus Christ—and another social structure known as the *ekklēsia*—not one sanctioned by the status quo. Yet we must remember that Paul also wrote those famous words in Romans 13: "Let every person be subject to the governing authorities." And we must remember that it was a system of belief and practice that suited the empire all too well, providing a new ideology of empire from Constantine onwards. Given a choice of opposing empire or accommodating, Paul could not decide.

It is this ambivalence that Calvin inherits from Paul. In the same way that Paul dithers between radicalism and reaction, so also does Calvin. In the same way that Paul equivocates over the radical possibilities of this new message and his tendency to recoil, so also does Calvin. And in the same way that Paul has the option of breaking through decisively or retreating to safer ground, so also does Calvin.

Conclusion

What If? Calvin and the Spirit of Revolution

This conclusion is more speculative than the earlier parts of my study. I ask, What if we let loose the revolutionary strain of Calvin's theology and politics? Rather than staying with the various tensions I have been tracing, I would like to free the radical potential from Calvin's own hesitations and qualifications, from his own innate conservatism. Is it possible that within Calvin are the seeds of a truly radical reading that is both theological and political? After a summary of my argument in the book thus far, I pursue such a reading through the four topics of Bible, grace, freedom, and politics.

SUMMARY

Throughout this book my argument has been that Calvin struggles with a theological tension that has wide-ranging political implications. It is a tension between radical and conservative elements in his thought, or between the revolutionary and reactionary. Calvin keeps opening up radical possibilities in all manner of theological corners, possibilities that he then sets out carefully to contain in a conservative fashion. I have used various images for this struggle, but the one I like most is that of the revolutionary cat in the theological bag. Time and again, Calvin opens up the mouth of the bag, however small the opening may be, and the cat glimpses daylight and makes a dash for freedom. Each time,

Calvin manages to clasp the bag shut again before the cat can break out or even sink a claw or fang into those firm hands wrapped around the mouth of the bag. Now, Calvin may open the bag deliberately or not so deliberately, for sometimes the radical possibility is an unintended consequence of a position he has taken. But every effort to shove the cat back in and tie up the mouth of the bag is definitely intentional. After all, Calvin's default position is a conservative one, and many have read and understood him in precisely this fashion. He would dearly like the world to be so; the problem is that the Bible he reads and the position he espouses are not so neat and tidy. As we have seen, in the end, in the last chapter of the *Institutes,* Calvin does indeed let the revolutionary cat out of the bag. Here it is a conjunction of both his theological position (all of us, rulers included, are fallen creatures and must obey God) and his high view of Scripture (it proceeds from the mouth of God and is not dependent on human beings). Against his better judgment, both make it perfectly clear that believers are not to obey ungodly rulers.

In a little more detail, I explored this argument over six phases. The first really set out to establish some context. Here the Peasants' Revolt of 1525, the Münster Revolution of 1534–1535, and the *Affaire des Placards* of 1534 provided a perpetual rumble of radical unrest that was both theological and political. Calvin sets out in the preface addressed to Francis I of France (who had an up-close and personal encounter with the aforesaid placards) to distance himself from these radicals. His rhetorical strategy is to set up one extreme, the revolutionary Reformers, over against another, the corrupt legalism of Rome. Between these two he then sets out what appears to be a moderate path. While it is a brilliant exercise of rhetoric (one that I have used to great effect on more than one occasion), it also conceals the fact that Calvin actually protests a little too much. In the great detail of what he does not do, Calvin provides a comprehensive description of revolution: it removes kings from power, throws out the laws, overturns the lawcourts, disturbs the peace, pays no heed to privilege and inherited status, and turns everything topsy-turvy.

In turning to the themes of Calvin's own work, I began with Calvin's approach to the Bible. Here I tried to characterize Calvin's view of the Bible in terms of a hot-air balloon: all the while wanting to lift off into higher and purer reaches, it remains tethered to the ground. Calvin is as keen as can be to remove the Bible from human hands, especially the Church on one side, and the radical anarchists on the other. The Bible is out of the reach of grasping human hands, for no human being can determine what is in the Bible or what it says. In order to make this argument stick, Calvin tries a number of moves (the Bible comes before the church; it is an "auto-faith" document), but he settles on the idea that it proceeds from the mouth of God and should therefore not be questioned. However, before it manages to float away completely, he ties it back down to earth by means of the Holy Spirit. This third person of the Trinity witnesses to the divine and unquestioned status of the Bible. All in all, this is a very high view of Scripture. The catch is that it may lead in two directions: the well-trodden conservative path in which the Bible is not to be questioned; or the lesser-known path of radical critiques of oppression, visions of new forms of living, and stories of revolutionary change. God may often be a conservative, but every now and then he turns out to be a refreshing revolutionary.

From there I moved on to consider the great theme of grace. What is striking about Calvin's treatment of grace is a direct ratio: the more sinful and reprobate we are, the more radical grace must become. Since we can do no more than grovel pitiably, all the work of salvation falls to God's grace. So we find Calvin writing of the abolition and destruction of our old selves and the complete replacement with something new that comes from within the very being of God. Any number of metaphors might have been used here, but Calvin draws his image from Ezekiel: God removes the old, corrupt, and sinful heart of stone and replaces it with an entirely new heart of flesh. Calvin draws deeply on the ideas of conversion, transformation, re-creation, and revolution. At this point, however, he begins to reel grace in again. It has had a good play, threatening to become very radical indeed, but now he lays down the rules as to how grace can in fact work. It must follow a set path: due to sin, grace grants the gift of faith, which then enables belief in God, which then leads to a righteous and good will. And rhetorically we find Calvin organizing his discussion in terms of neat pairs and categories, all effectively directing grace down the channel he has created for it. Then he makes that famous move from what may best be called the democracy of depravity to the aristocracy of salvation; grace applies only to those sacred aristocrats. In light of all this—allowing grace to have its head and then hauling it back in—I suggested that here we have the first instance of what I called the "revolutionary paradox," namely, the tendency for radical impulses to fall back all too easily on reaction and repression.

From grace it was a short step to Christian freedom, a topic Calvin found both absolutely necessary and very tricky. Veer too far one way, and he ends up in the Scylla of anarchist radicals such as those at Münster; veer the other way, and he risks being sucked into the legalism of

Charybdis's whirlpool. What does he do? He sets about in his accustomed fashion to stipulate exactly what types of freedom are meant and thereby permissible for the Christian: freedom from the law and for Christ; freedom from outer in favor of inner compulsion; and freedom from external observance. The problem for Calvin is that these three categories don't really restrict freedom at all: they actually open up even more radical vistas, for freedom from the law, from outer compulsion, and outer observance were and are taken by liberals as basic to the drives for human rights and universal democracy. So Calvin comes in hard with another distinction: spiritual versus temporal, or private versus public. Christian freedom is strictly a private, spiritual affair and has nothing to do with the temporal. Later he will bring these two back together, but for now they serve his purpose of keeping freedom out of the domain of politics. In tracing the way Calvin ends up steering closer to the Charybdis of legalism, I also sought an answer to the paradox of Calvinist legalism.

The Bible's authority and the tensions over freedom and grace turn up in a slightly different light with the last chapter of the *Institutes*, the famous one on "civil order" (perhaps he should have named it "civil disorder"). Calvin concludes, rather explosively, that God actually expects one not to obey ungodly rulers, even if they have been divinely appointed. Or rather, this is what Calvin finds in the Bible, which, we should remember, comes from the lips of God. The path to that point is a difficult one for Calvin. In the last chapter of the *Institutes* (bk. 4, chap. 20, which remained unchanged over many editions), he begins by distinguishing between anarchy and tyranny. How does one avoid both in the search for a properly Christian polity? To begin with, Calvin waters down the distinction of the temporal and the spiritual that was so necessary for his discussion of freedom. The two are in fact connected, for the task of earthly rulers is to ensure true religion. The connection between these two realms also opens up the argument (drawn from the Bible) that we common people should obey our rulers, for they have been appointed by God. And if so, we should even obey them when they manifestly rule unjustly, for that must be seen as chastisement for our sins. But then Calvin faces a problem: rulers are removed from power with frightening regularity in the Bible. So he proposes the solution that such acts may be carried out by God or his divinely appointed agents (whether they know it or not). Among these (the knowing ones) may be found magistrates, whose task is to curb, check, and occasionally punish an ungodly ruler. However, just when this neat scheme is in place, Calvin breaks out in the last section to state that given the choice between obeying an unjust ruler or obeying God, we must obey God. No qualifications, no efforts to mediate a difficult position; because rulers are sinful creatures like us and will have a propensity to do the wrong thing, they will tend to tyranny, decreeing ungodly laws and forcing the faithful to obey. In these cases, the faithful are duty bound to obey God alone. The careful structures of his previous argument seem all but undone (although there are many that try to put Humpty Dumpty together again).

The final chapter migrated to a neighboring territory. I set out to see whether these tensions were of Calvin's own making, or whether he had picked them up from somewhere else. That somewhere turned out to be the Bible. This was no great surprise, for Calvin's high view of Scripture led him to lean heavily on that text. But what is fascinating about his engagement with the Bible is that although he sets out to read it in a univocal fashion (after all, it is supposed to issue from the mouth of God), he often ends up recognizing despite himself that it is a multivocal text. This second level of reading is not altogether a conscious or intentional one on Calvin's part, but that makes it only more revealing. With this argument tucked into my belt, I set off to explore the multivalent and multivocal texts of the Bible, especially the Letters of Paul. Here I found a whole series of oppositions at work—Jew and Greek, male and female, slave and free, flesh and spirit, Adam and Christ, death and life, sin and redemption, works and faith, law and grace, and so on. Paul struggles with these oppositions, tackling them in different ways. My point was that Calvin picked up these oppositions in his careful reading of Paul and then reshaped them with his own emphases. There was one further step in my argument, and that was to suggest that both Calvin and Paul provided imaginary resolutions of their socioeconomic situations. With his emphasis on the abolition of, transformation of, and transition from works into faith, law into grace, and death into life, Calvin both mapped and provided a narrative to assist people in navigating the drawn-out and violent transition from feudalism into capitalism. In this respect, Calvin's situation is analogous to Paul's, where we find the seismic and extraordinarily violent shift taking place from an older Sacred Economy to the slave-based economic system characteristic of Greece and then Rome. Like Calvin, Paul too provides a map and a way of coping with such a change, although he does it with great ambivalence. Paul struggled with the wild and radical edge of the message he was propounding. When he saw that some of his listeners and readers wanted to take his message of a law-free gospel much further, he began a series of containment actions in order to restrict such logical conclusions. In all these respects, Calvin inherits an insight or two.

In light of all this, what might a radical Calvin look like? The four themes are the central ones of Bible, grace, freedom, and politics. Before I dive in, let me provide a schematic diagram of what I want to do with each one:

a. Bible
High view → radical Bible (criticism, community, and insurrection)
b. Grace
Radical depravity → radical grace
(where conversion = transformation = re-creation = revolution)
c. Freedom
Freedom from law/outer compulsion/external observance →
freedom in *both* spiritual and temporal domains
d. Politics
Obey ungodly rulers? → Obey only God.

BIBLE

The formula (see above) for a radical Bible comes out of Calvin himself. Or rather, it is one path that emerges from Calvin's doctrine of Scripture, a path I choose to take. But then this formula assumes the argument I developed in chapter 2, which I represented in terms of the following diagram:

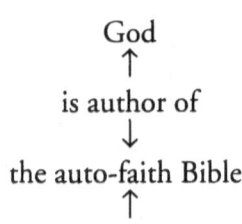

God
↑
is author of
↓
the auto-faith Bible,
↑
which is witnessed to by
the Holy Spirit, who gives the link with
↓
human beings, who have no authority over the Bible.

Or to come up with the briefest statement possible: Calvin has a very high view of the Bible. Now, as I pointed out towards the close of chapter 2, this high view has led many down the well-worn path of conservative positions on the Bible: it is from the mouth of God and is thus inerrant and infallible (just like God). But there is another path less well trodden but far more interesting. It begins by recognizing as metaphors Calvin's talk of the Bible coming from the mouth and lips of God. It then moves on to see what the function of those metaphors might be: they are metaphors of significance and importance, even unto matters of life and death. It follows that if one takes such a high view of the Bible, then one should take very seriously indeed the rebukes of economic oppression, visions of radical collective living, promises of final judgment for oppressors and justice for the oppressed, and stories of openness and inclusiveness. Even more, I am thoroughly intrigued by the way such a high view can lead to the image of a revolutionary God. Let us explore some of these texts more closely.

The condemnations of economic oppression are found throughout the Bible, placed in the mouths of Moses, the Prophets, and Jesus, and turn up with surprising regularity in the Law and Wisdom sayings. Such texts still inspire and give motivation to those who want to critique and overcome the differences and injustices of wealth, power, and privilege. We find the most sustained criticisms in the mouths of prophets.

For example, Amos fires off some forceful condemnations:

> Thus says the LORD:
> For three transgressions of Israel,
>   and for four, I will not revoke the punishment;
> because they sell the righteous for silver,
>   and the needy for a pair of sandals—
> they who trample the head of the poor into the dust of the earth.
>   (Amos 2:6–7)

The overwhelming image is of trampling the poor into the dust. Here the condemnation concerns the selling of the righteous and the needy. It may be a reference to slavery, especially debt slavery, but notice how the terms for "righteous" and "needy" merge into one another: "They sell the righteous for silver, / and the needy for a pair of sandals." "Righteous" is a bad translation, since it now tends to designate an overly pious and self-righteous person. I would suggest that "just" is better, or (my own preference) the "uncorrupted," those who do not engage in corrupt and deceitful practices. Another text from Amos spells out such corruption and deceit in some detail:

> Hear this, you who trample upon the needy,
>   and bring to ruin the poor of the land,
> saying, "When will the new moon be over,
>   so that we may sell grain; and the sabbath,
>   so that we may offer wheat for sale?
> We will make the ephah small and the shekel great,
>   and practice deceit with false balances,
> buying the poor for silver
>   and the needy for a pair of sandals,
>   and selling the sweepings of the wheat."
>
> (Amos 8:4–6)

Bothered by the waste of time at religious festivals, the corrupt make use of false weights (reducing the ephah) and false balances, sell waste products as though they were the real thing (the sweepings of the wheat), so that they can take even more from the poor and needy. (Nothing seems to have changed: I often wonder what those strange substances are in the bread we buy today.) They seek whatever strategy they can find to bring the poor and needy into debt slavery.[1]

Another who rings out with Amos-like condemnations is Isaiah:

> The LORD enters into judgment
>   with the elders and princes of his people:
> It is you who have devoured the vineyard;
>   the spoil of the poor is in your houses.
> What do you mean by crushing my people,
>   by grinding the face of the poor?
> says the Lord GOD of hosts.
>
> (Isa. 3:14–15)

This text is very close to the first one I quoted from Amos. Those trampled upon in Amos now are crushed and have their faces ground down. Notice here too that "the people" and "the poor" merge with one another: "What do you mean by crushing my people / by grinding the face of the poor?" The "poor" are God's people, "my people," and the rulers are in for some trouble. As for those rulers, or more accurately elders and chieftains, they are the guilty ones. It is precisely

---

1. In his commentary on both these passages (1846, 179-83, 361–67), Calvin first struggles to get over a couple of hurdles: Why doesn't Amos criticize their "superstitions" first, and why doesn't he mention the common people? Once he is over the first hurdle (such criticism has its place, he points out), he launches into the "rapacity, avarice and cruelty" (183) of such oppression, especially if these elders and rulers maintained a pious exterior. He manages to get over the second hurdle by letting his more conservative side come to the fore: he assures himself that society must be very corrupt if such problems have actually gone beyond the common people and reached up to the ruling class.

those who command and demand honor—whether through age and power—who are at fault.[2]

There are many other passages like this that come from those amorphous collections known as the Prophets. Elsewhere we find similar themes: Moses stands and calls on Pharaoh to "let my people go" (Exod. 5:1; Calvin 1852b, 112–13). In the New Testament, Jesus condemns the rich and powerful, propagates an antiestablishment and anticlerical position, identifies with the poor and oppressed, and loves a communal life with the disciples, who gave up all to join the group. Well-known sayings still have an edge: "It is easier for a camel to go through the eye of a needle than for someone who is rich to enter the kingdom of God" (Mark 10:25). Or the words of the Son of Man, when he identifies with the poor and hungry in the parable of the Sheep and the Goats: "I was hungry and you gave me food, I was thirsty and you gave me something to drink, I was a stranger and you welcomed me, I was naked and you gave me clothing, I was sick and you took care of me, I was in prison and you visited me" (Matt. 25:35–36). If we take seriously the high view of Scripture touted by Calvin, then we can't avoid the need to take notice of these outright condemnations of grinding the poor and needy into the dust. But it is important to keep the economic and social focus of these texts: they expose and decry economic and social exploitation.

A further theme that emerges from the Bible is that of communal or communist living—understood in the original sense of the term. Quite simply, according to Calvin's high view of Scripture, if God says communist living is desirable, then it must be so. Despite murmurings about celestial pies and futile schemes for improvement, we cannot escape the enduring power of the image of communal living that appears in the Acts of the Apostles. This has been a founding and enabling myth for Christian communism. It comes from Acts 2:44–45: "And all who believed were together and had all things in common; they would sell their possessions and goods and distribute the proceeds to all, as any had need." An inspiration for generations of Christian communists and socialists, this text from Acts is expanded in Acts 4:32–35 with its talk of having everything in common and the distribution to any who had need:

> Now the whole group of those who believed were of one heart and soul, and no one claimed private ownership of any possessions, but everything they owned was held in common. With great power the

---

[2]. Note here that in his commentary on Isaiah, Calvin agrees and doesn't try to explain away these sharp condemnations of the rich and powerful (1850, 141–43).

apostles gave their testimony to the resurrection of the Lord Jesus, and great grace was upon them all. There was not a needy person among them, for as many as owned lands or houses sold them and brought the proceeds of what was sold. They laid it at the apostles' feet, and it was distributed to each as any had need.

In the face of explicit Christian communism in these texts, it is interesting to see what a range of scholars do with them. They argue that such communal activity was voluntary and only for a short time (during a festival) and by no means the "imposition" of a communist system. Or we find that such common living is applied to that new invention of the last couple of centuries, the nuclear family (which, by the way, cannot be found in the Bible). Not only is this a popular argument today, but it was also one that both Luther (1959, 363) and Calvin (1844a, 130–31, 190–93) put forward, who were desperate to avoid the communal interpretations of the Anabaptists and the abuses of Roman Catholic monasteries. Or as Calvin and later neo-orthodox readings suggested, the qualities of unity, love, and generosity are abstracted from the passage, and the actual practice is pushed into the background. In the last century the resistance to communism and the effect of the Cold War lies heavily on the interpretation of these texts. In reaction to claims by communist scholars such as Friedrich Engels (1990), Karl Kautsky (2001), and Rosa Luxemburg (2004) that these texts speak of an early Christian communism that has much in common with the communism we know, a wide range of scholars resisted such interpretations in the name of the private individual. So the historical possibility was undermined, the text spiritualized, or its sense diverted into acceptable forms of cooperation, such as the family or one's local church. In short, a wide range of interpreters sought to negate the text. If we take Calvin's high view of Scripture, then that is the last thing we should do.

A stronger image of what is required for communal life comes from the Hebrew Bible:

> What does the LORD require of you
> but to do justice, and to love kindness,
> and to walk humbly with your God?
> (Mic. 6:8)

Now, while this may seem rather simple, doing justice, loving kindness, and walking humbly comprise a tough standard for any collective or even individual life.[3] This is where the words of Isaiah join in, indicating what it means to live according to these three precepts:

> The Spirit of the Lord GOD is upon me,
> because the LORD has anointed me;
> he has sent me to bring good news to the oppressed,
> > to bind up the brokenhearted,
> to proclaim liberty to the captives,
> > and release to the prisoners;
> to proclaim the year of the LORD's favor,
> > and the day of vengeance of our God.
> > > (Isa. 61:1–2)

This text might be read as a direct follow-up from the condemnations I discussed in the previous section relating to oppression. Here the captives are to be set free and the prisoners released; the poor and brokenhearted are to hear good news. Not quite a detailed program for reform, but then it is a poetic text, and it would be enough to send an earthquake or two through any vested power. It does, however, hint at what is required for any viable collective living, namely, the end of exploitation and oppression, and that is a substantial and revolutionary move. It is not for nothing that the Gospel of Luke places this text in the mouth of Jesus when he is in the synagogue in Nazareth (Luke 4:18–19).

At this point we are squarely in the realm of apocalyptic stories about the return of God to set aright injustice, deliver the final judgment, and destroy evil. Much more could be said, but it is clear that the Bible has a distinctly radical line to it. But what we have with Calvin's high view of Scripture is a radical political view, condemning oppression, offering images of a communist life, and speaking of a radical judgment that will destroy the oppressors. Let me reiterate what that high view entails: it comes metaphorically from the mouth of God, it is the sole source for direction, and it upsets any human endeavor. The first two are relatively obvious, but what about the third? These sorts of texts create all sorts of problems for anyone who is politically or economically conservative. And Calvin is precisely one of these people. He too will need to be prepared to be surprised by his own doctrine of Scripture.

---

3. Unfortunately, in his commentaries on both the Amos and Isaiah passages, Calvin spiritualizes the text to refer to the inner life of faith (1847b, 342–43; 1853, 304–6).

CONCLUSION

GRACE

Radical depravity → radical grace
(where conversion = transformation = re-creation = revolution)

As far as grace is concerned, there are two angles we may pursue, one that may be expected at this point and the other not. The first involves simply releasing the brakes that Calvin has applied to grace with his various qualifications and careful efforts to channel it, while the second takes predestination head on and gives it a twist.

Before pursuing both elements, let us take a step back and consider the democracy of depravity. I have always liked the first point of traditional Calvinism: total depravity. Always good for a joke (I have always done my best to affirm . . .), it also has the advantage of being thoroughly realistic and thoroughly democratic.

On realism: the sad and sorry tale of human destructiveness, perpetual wars, the merest excuse for torture (as we have seen yet again most recently in the long-running invasions of Afghanistan and Iraq), and the alacrity with which people want to make a profit from wars— all these speak of the utter sinfulness of human beings. Add to this the tendency to seek power, to make one's neighbor suffer for one's own aggrandizement, and to exercise power brutally and effectively. Even more, one does not have to look too far to find the overwhelming push to drive wages down so that one may increase one's profit margin, to crush opponents, to remove hard-won gains by workers, to have scant regard for environmental concerns when they interfere with business, to make the poor suffer so the rich may live in luxury. Despite the overwhelming information concerning the effects of human industrial activity (especially of the capitalist variety) on the natural ecology of which we are a part, human beings seem singularly incapable of making the necessary changes to avoid some sort of catastrophe. (As I daily count the coal ships waiting to come into harbor and to load at my home port in Newcastle, Australia, I become more and more an environmental skeptic—skeptical that anything will be done.) At a more personal level, poisoned relations between family members are only far too common (same story, different family); children are regularly and systematically abused (emotionally and physically) by parents in that strange institution known as the nuclear family; and it seems a given that we hurt the one we love. Totally sinful, completely reprobate, utterly depraved? Absolutely.

The problem for so many is that such a doctrine goes against a sense that we are worth something, that we are good in some way or other. To tell someone that she or he is a worthless, depraved, and despicable sinner, no better than the scum in the security prison, is generally regarded as an insult. But this doctrine is also radically democratic, and here I move a little beyond Calvin. It is by no means a new point, but well worth emphasizing and broadcasting as loudly as possible: utter sinfulness is universal. That means that all human beings are in the same boat and that no one is better than anyone else. It is, if you like, a democracy of the lowest common denominator: we all live in the same cesspool.

Even though it is not an attractive form of democracy, it does have the huge advantage of upsetting the rich and powerful (as well as the would-be rich and powerful). To tell an aristocrat that he is as worthless before God as either the filthy peasant or the uncultured bourgeois was potentially revolutionary. Or in our own day, to tell the filthy-rich stock market speculator that her fortune and power count for nothing before God would not be the best way to win friends and influence people. Or to admit to ourselves that all "diligence, insight, understanding, and carefulness"—in short, the "keenness of reason, which we count the most precious gift of all" (*Inst.* 2.2.25; *OS* 3:267.32–35)—are misdirected and useless is to admit a lot for those of us who make a living from that intellect. Those who shared this position with Calvin, such as Martin Luther and John Wesley, did not find the privileged or intellectual classes were overly enthused. Indeed, many were outraged at the preposterous suggestion that they and the servants were all on the same footing with God.

If radical depravity is deeply democratic, then why is grace not so in Calvin's thought? We may wish that it might have been, that he had seen that utter reliance on the grace of God for anything that might count as good is potentially democratic, that justification by faith rather than works removes any basis for privilege, but he did not argue this. Instead, what we find is what I called the aristocracy of salvation. In the chapter on grace, I argued that this contradiction between democratic depravity and aristocratic salvation is one manifestation of the contradiction of grace in Calvin's thought. Calvin was, after all, no democrat. Remember that he believed the best form of government was an aristocracy with strong populist tendencies.

At this point, the twist I promised earlier comes into play: What if the distinction between the elect and the damned is one that each of us contains within ourselves?[4] Calvin loved to distinguish between groups: the Anabaptists caused him grief on one side, while the Church of Rome troubled him on the other. With predestination we have a distinct group who are certain of their salvation, which has been decreed from eternity; this group stands over against the other, larger group of those who are eternally damned. But what happens when we link this doctrine with another feature of Calvin's thought, namely, the turn inward and the valuing of the private individual? In this case, the line between election and damnation runs right through the center of our being, or of our souls, as Calvin would put it. While the issues of eternal decrees and certainty of salvation and damnation are troubled by such a move, it does open an unexpected democratic angle.

There are more radical possibilities for grace, especially in light of the equation I suggested earlier: grace is the theological version of the political revolution, and vice versa. Calvin emphasizes the radical, life-changing action of grace in no uncertain terms. As the cluster of Latin terms makes perfectly clear, it completely abolishes (*aboleo*) the life of old, effects a turning around or conversion (*converse* and *convertio*), and brings about a transformation (*transformo*) and re-creation (*renovo*). In short, grace is a thoroughly revolutionary affair. Yes, of course, most would say—at a personal level (after all, Calvin gives a good deal of attention to such spiritual matters). However, as soon as we think of these terms in a political sense, to abolish completely, turn around, transform, and re-create all speak of political revolution.

There is, however, a further and somewhat unexpected outcome of revolutionary grace. A crucial feature of such grace is that the agency comes from outside human beings (Calvin attributes such agency completely to God). Since we can do no good work, let alone anything that will help in our salvation, all of that must come from God's grace, that is, entirely from outside any human agency. This is a radical position from the heart of Calvin: human beings are put on the side and thoroughly decentered. There surely is plenty within Calvin's texts that indicate anthropocentrism, but there is also a strong drive that pushes human beings off to the side. It is high time we became peripheral, he says, for we have made an unremitting mess of things, and the more we try to fix them, the worse it gets. This is not an anthropocentric world or universe, he is telling us. Once again, Calvin challenges

---

4. I develop this suggestion from Lucien Goldmann's *The Hidden God* (1959; 1964), a patchy and idiosyncratic study of Jansenism that has moments of sheer brilliance. See the fuller discussion of Goldmann in my *Criticism of Religion* (Boer in press).

human assumptions about superiority and importance. A perfectly logical extension of that position is to expand it into environmental matters. Is not much of the environmental destruction we now experience increasingly around us the result of human assumptions of superiority or indeed separateness from the natural world? Calvin actually enables a view that decenters humanity in radical fashion: we are not the most important part of creation.

When we take Calvin's anthropofugal drive further, then the following point emerges: the agency for (revolutionary) change may well come from outside human beings. We like to think that all hitherto revolutionary transformations have been the result of human activity: invention of tools, the wheel, weapons, agriculture, animal husbandry, industry, sliced bread, and even changes from one socioeconomic system to another (slavery to feudalism and thence to capitalism). But what if major changes did not always result from human agency? Calvin would direct us to God, but I would also suggest that the principle (outside human agency) also means that nature may be an agent of revolutionary change. Nature is, after all, God's creation. Lest my readers think I have finally gone off the deep end, or that I have lapsed into some form of pantheism or panentheism, let me use Calvin's impeccable logic. We tend to feel that we can fix things if they are broken, but Calvin reminds us that we are chronically unable to do so. The agency for that must come from beyond us. The principle here is deceptively simple: in an anthropocentric world, revolutionary change must come from beyond human control. Or in Calvin's terms, we can't save ourselves.

FREEDOM

Freedom from law/outer compulsion/external observance →
freedom in both spiritual and temporal domains

What if we let freedom, *libertas*, have its head? It seems like a trick question, for the way to do so seems disarmingly simple. All we need to do is take Calvin's position on freedom and remove its checks. He argues for freedom from the law (and for Christ), freedom from outer coercion in favor of inner compulsion, and freedom from concern over external observances. But he restricts the radical potential of freedom by means of a sharp distinction between private spiritual matters and public temporal ones: Christian liberty belongs to the former and not to the latter. Perhaps the best phrase for capturing all of this is not so much Christian freedom as freedom on a leash—*freedom on a tight leash*. The problem is that freedom tugs and pants and puffs at that leash, trying to break free. By contrast, if we let freedom go, if we wanted a fully radical freedom, then we would need to insist that Christian freedom applies to *both* the spiritual and temporal realms. In fact, we would need to argue that the two are indeed connected, as Calvin does in the last chapter of the *Institutes*.

Yet this move raises another question: What would such a freedom look like? Unfortunately, the word "freedom" has been badly tainted in our own time. We have, for example, the perpetual propaganda of the "free market," which really means that the various capitalists may exploit workers and the environment, sell shoddy products, and try to swallow one another up without any legislative interference from the governments of nation-states or indeed from global judiciaries. Here we have freedom *from* what is variously called red tape, rules and regulations, taxes, environmental concerns, tariffs, and so on. And we have freedom *for* unbridled and anything-goes competition. Needless to say, there is actually no such thing as "free trade," for one will always stumble across at least one rule, namely, that which legislates free trade in the first place.

Or we find the constant push to connect the capitalist global market with "democracy." The guilty parties on this count are Friedrich von Hayek's *The Constitution of Liberty* (1960) and Milton Friedman's *Capitalism and Freedom* (2002), along with a host of even lesser minds. Grand efforts to rivet "liberty" onto capitalism, these works became the ideological underpinnings for the renewed wave of laissez-faire economics in the later decades of the twentieth century, although it is less popular these days with the massive economic collapse of 2008–2009. Leave the market be, goes the argument, and it will regulate itself. Even more, a free market is the guarantee of democratic freedom. Let the "free market" in, and democracy will soon follow. So we continue to hear the tireless propaganda that the two are joined at the hip, even as the story becomes more and more tarnished as yet another state finds "freedom" imposed upon it with the barrel of a gun, or that such a "free market" leads to only more impoverishment (see Surin in press). In this case "freedom" came to mean the global dominance of a capitalist market and the imposition of parliamentary democracy.

Or freedom has come to mean personal and individual freedom, something for which Calvin is partly to blame. Now, Calvin would shiver in disgust at what such inner, personal freedom has come to mean: I can do what I want with my body and with my life and achieve what I want. As I argued in the chapter on freedom, this notion of freedom comes as part of the ideological package known as the private individual. Once upon a time, such an idea of freedom was deeply radical and even revolutionary. The privileged aristocracy of an old and fading order once trembled to their cores at claims to individual freedom, universal suffrage, and the "rights of man." At that time, it was the bourgeoisie flexing its increasingly toned and bulking muscles, claiming personal freedom as its slogan, and waging a long and often bloody revolutionary war with the old ruling class. The sad truth is that such an idea of freedom has ceased to be revolutionary. Instead, it has vigorously claimed the personal and private as a nonpolitical and even conservative space.

So what does such personal freedom mean today? It means I have freedom of choice—the type of bread I buy from the racks at the bakery or supermarket, the endless types of jam I can put on it, or indeed cheese or peanut butter or . . . We are accustomed to the idea of free choice, for it is touted day by day and minute by minute. We are free to choose what doctor to see, what school to send our children to, what house to buy, and what town in which to live. And in case governments come a little too close to the "nanny state," we have energetic civil liberties groups and consumer-advocacy groups ready to leap to the defense of so-called freedom of choice.

Freedom also means liberation. Here our path splits into two. One leads down the track towards individual "liberty." For example, the liberation of women can mean the liberty of women to be free individuals who may make choices over their lives. This meaning is strongest in places where the ideology of liberalism has played a greater role. I think here of the United States, with its close connection to the French proclamation of "liberty, equality, and fraternity." The other path bends towards the left and sees liberation as collective freedom from oppression and exploitation—characteristic of places as various as Latin America, with liberation theology; of former colonies where indigenous peoples seek a modicum of recompense for past injustices; or indeed of Scandinavia, with its strong social democratic tradition. In each case, liberation is much a collective agenda and experience. As Jorunn Økland and I point out (Økland and Boer 2008), because of its history a country like Norway went straight from being a precapitalist tribal society to a postcapitalist tribal society. It virtually bypassed the saturation in individualism so characteristic of places like the United States.

In fact, it seems as though everyone wants freedom: the liberation theologians cry out for it, usually in close connection with justice; the Maoist rebels in Nepal have fought for it; Western teenagers want it, usually with a driver's license; adults are meant to have it, but with a good dose of responsibility; women, gays, lesbians, and indigenous peoples struggle for it; socialists and anarchists long for true freedom; consumers have it in abundance, supposedly; the people of Iraq wanted it, apparently. A little overused, is it not?

So what does freedom in both spiritual and temporal domains really mean? I could trot out the usual points: freedom from oppression, degradation, and discrimination in terms of class, income, gender, ethnicity, religion. I may also add a few from Calvin himself: freedom from ungodly rulers and from external compulsion. But let me put it as follows.

Here I draw on Lenin's (1975, 623; see Žižek 2001, 112–14) distinction between formal and actual freedom. Quite simply, actual freedom is the possibility and ability to step outside a particular situation. It is suspicious of and discards that thick cluster of presuppositions that constitute the absolute horizon of thought and action, the point beyond which we cannot normally think or act. By contrast, formal freedom is a constrained or limited freedom whose boundaries are determined by our situation. We might think we have an unlimited range of choices, but we do not. Our apparent freedom operates within the terms carefully established by the existing relations of power. It is a forced freedom. The difference is massive: actual freedom is not the choice between two or more options within a given situation, but the choice of changing the very situation itself. For example, my ability to choose from what appear to be a wide variety of shoes in numerous shoe shops is really formal freedom: faced with such a bewildering array of choices, I fail to see that the political-economic structure that generates the types of shoes available and the shops from which I can buy them has already set the boundaries of the range of choice itself. I can choose what shoes to buy, but I cannot choose to blow up these shoe shops or eradicate them and the system that supports them. I can choose all I like, as long as I don't "rock the boat."

Lenin had the knack of asking whose interest is served by the claim of "freedom." He would say, "Freedom—yes, but for whom? To do what?" (see Žižek 2001, 114). And the purpose of such a question is to keep open the possibility of real choice, of an actual freedom. To take it one step further, such an actual, unforced freedom can change the coordinates of formal freedom. It is the freedom to discard the very system in which we live and begin to construct a new one, or as Calvin would put it, to abolish the old and re-create the new, to cut out the heart of stone and replace it with a new one of flesh. It is, in short, revolutionary freedom.

POLITICS

The formula for the final of the four great themes in Calvin's work is as follows: Obey ungodly rulers? → Obey only God. On this matter it is not so difficult to draw out the revolutionary potential of Calvin's deliberations on what is quaintly called *civil order*. All it requires me to do is give my assent to the last section of the last chapter of the *Institutes*: Follow your rulers, but only if they obey God. Let me translate this: It is our duty to disregard and disobey any government, any ruler, indeed any socioeconomic system that does not measure up to a higher code of requirements for which we use the name "God." Or as Calvin puts it in the last words of the *Institutes*: "We have been redeemed by Christ at so great a price as our redemption cost him, so that we should not enslave ourselves to the wicked desires of men—much less be subject to their impiety" [1 Cor. 7:23] (*Inst.* 4.20.32; *OS* 5:502.28–31). Rulers are, after all, depraved and impious men, just like the rest of us.

However, as we saw in chapter 5, Calvin doesn't get to this point without a struggle. He moves from asserting that we should obey our rulers, no matter how tyrannical, to saying that only God and/or his appointed agents may punish such demonic rulers. But then, just as he is outlining how magistrates are one of these special appointees, there to curb and check ungodly rulers, he breaks out and lets both the Bible and the rest of his theological system come into play. The result: in a final rush, the asserts that we owe them no allegiance whatsoever if they don't rule correctly, that is, in a godly fashion.

In my earlier discussion I pointed out that Calvin does not actually tell people that they are permitted to overthrow rulers—and by "people" I mean the democratic mass of whom Calvin is somewhat afraid. By contrast, God and an appointed agent may do just about anything to a tyrant: they may restrain or curb (*coerceo*), punish (*animadverto*), inflict recompense on (*poenas sumo*), take up arms against (*arma sumo*), and deliver people from (*eximo*) a tyrannical ruler. But the most that the people (you and me, or most readers at least) can do is refuse to do what the ruling class tells us to do. We might call this mass civil disobedience.

Not quite a revolutionary overthrow on its own; not quite the tearing up of the law books, upending the judges' benches, causing a ruckus in that leafy neighborhood, seizing the media outlets, and throwing the corrupt ruling class in prison. That, after all, is for God and his agents. But let us see what happens when we combine all three possibilities: mass civil disobedience, the avenging hand of an agent of God, and the direct punishment of God. Not a bad combination, if you ask me. Widespread civil disobedience is a powerful tool indeed, as Gandhi showed in the struggle for Indian independence, or as the various revolutions in Eastern Europe in the late 1980s showed. Throw in an agent who may play a more active role, such as deliver people from an oppressor, and God himself, who may tear power out of their hands, and we have an effective revolutionary combination at work.

I must admit that there is one item that bothers me about this formulation: God's role, or rather, the conviction that God is on our side. It is not that I have anything against God as a revolutionary (the idea is actually very appealing), but human beings have claimed to be God's avenging arm a few too many times in history for one to be all that comfortable with the claim. This claim has been and continues to be made by revolutionary groups on the one hand, and by the cruelest tyrants as well as lesser despots on the other. If we take the tyrants and despots for a moment, then the number of divine agents claiming to act on behalf of God over the last few centuries is a very long list indeed. Did not the Dutch, Spanish, Portuguese, Danish, English, and most recently American empires all claim to be agents of God? Did not the absolute and not-so-absolute monarchs of Germany, Denmark, France, and Spain all claim this status? Did they and do they not still use such a belief to justify ousting the odd ruler of a state with whom they were not so happy? The latest in a long line of ousted tyrants at the hands of God's self-appointed agent is Saddam Hussein. And did those responsible for deposing him not feel that they were obeying God in doing so?

There are two lines that might be taken in response to this problem. The first may be called a worldly wise cynicism and the second a need to take sides. The wise and very secular argument is to be profoundly suspicious of any claim to divine sanction and support. Such suspicion usually takes the form of the following principle: As soon as someone claims to represent God or claims that God is a guarantee for their hold on truth, we must be extremely wary, for we can be reasonably certain that neither God nor the truth is to be found there. It matters not who makes such a claim, whether it is the most callous and calculating despot or the most idealistic revolutionary out to make the world a better place. I have much sympathy with this position, for it is a good example of what I have elsewhere called theological suspicion (see Boer 2007c).

The second way of dealing with this problem is to be wary of the way the previous position may be an excuse for inaction. For some reason I am unhappy with the preceding argument, no matter how appealing it seems. Yes, everyone will nod, tyrants and zealots who claim to have God on their side are highly suspect. The problem is that all too often the need to step back and be suspicious of claims concerning divine guidance functions as a reason to avoid taking sides. The world is going to pot; human beings are totally corrupt; any movement to make the world a better place ends up making it worse; again and again efforts to overcome tyranny end up being even more oppressive and tyrannical; and the claims by tyrants or revolutionaries to have God on their side are deluded at best or megalomaniacal at worst— these and other reasons are usually put forward in order to avoid taking sides. What I like about Calvin is that he is not a fence-sitter; he clearly takes sides, whether we like the side he takes or not. In this case, Calvin is not merely a supporter of the status quo, whether king or magistrate or whoever he suggests must be obeyed. Nor is he merely a supporter of those who offer rulers mass disobedience, or indeed of agents who overthrow ungodly rulers. No, Calvin comes out against tyranny and oppression. Or rather, the part of Calvin true to his own theological impulse advocated such a position. It is these tyrants against whom he advocated civil disobedience, from whom he called for deliverance, and whose power he sought to be removed. And if any of those exercising civil disobedience or delivering people from an oppressor should become a tyrant in turn, then the same principle applies.

Bibliography

Agamben, Giorgio. 2000. *Il tempo che resta: Un commento alla Lettera ai Romani*. Turin: Bollati Boringhieri.
———. 2005. *The Time That Remains: A Commentary on the Letter to the Romans*. Trans. P. Dailey. Stanford, CA: Stanford University Press.
Aichele, George. 2001. *The Control of Biblical Meaning: Canon as a Semiotic Mechanism*. Harrisburg, PA: Trinity Press International.
Allen, J. W. A. 1941. *A History of Political Thought in the Sixteenth Century*. 2nd ed. London: Methuen.
Althusser, Louis. 1971. *Lenin and Philosophy and Other Essays*. Trans. B. Brewster. New York: Monthly Review Press.
Anderson, Perry. 1974. *Passages from Antiquity to Feudalism*. London: New Left Books.
———. 1979. *Lineages of the Absolutist State*. London: Verso.
Astruc, Jean. 1999. *Conjectures sur la Genèse*. Ed. P. Fibert. Paris: Agnès Viénot Editions.
Badiou, Alain. 1997. *Saint-Paul: La fondation de l'universalisme*. Paris: Presses universitaires de France.
———. 2003. *Saint Paul: The Foundation of Universalism*. Trans. R. Brassier. Stanford, CA: Stanford University Press.
Bendix, Reinhard. 1998. *Max Weber: An Intellectual Portrait*. London: Routledge.
Benedict, Philip. 2002. *Christ's Churches Purely Reformed: A Social History of Calvinism*. New Haven, CT: Yale University Press.
Berthoud, Garielle. 1973. *Antoine Marcourt: Réformateur et pamphlétaire du "Livre des Marchans" aux placards de 1534*. Paris: Droz.
Biéler, André. 1964. *The Social Humanism of Calvin*. Trans. P. Fuhrmann. Richmond, VA: John Knox Press.
———. 2006. *Calvin's Economic and Social Thought*. Trans. J. Greig. Geneva: World Alliance of Reformed Churches.
Blanton, Ward, and Hent De Vries, eds. Forthcoming. *Paul in Philosophy and Culture*. Chicago: University of Chicago Press.
Bloch, Ernst. 1969. *Thomas Münzer als Theologe der Revolution*. 2nd ed. 17 vols. Vol. 2, *Ernst Bloch Werkausgabe*. Frankfurt am Main: Suhrkamp.
———. 1972. *Atheism in Christianity: The Religion of the Exodus and the Kingdom*. Trans. J. T. Swann. New York: Herder & Herder.
Boer, Roland. 2006. On Fables and Truths. *Angelaki* 11 (2): 107–16.

———. 2007a. The Conundrums of Giorgio Agamben: A Commentary on *A Commentary to the Letter to the Romans*. *Sino-Christian Studies* 3:1-26.

———. 2007b. *Criticism of Heaven: On Marxism and Theology*, Historical Materialism Book Series. Leiden: E. J. Brill.

———. 2007c. *Rescuing the Bible*. Oxford: Blackwell.

———. 2007d. The Sacred Economy of Ancient "Israel." *The Scandinavian Journal of the Old Testament* 21 (1):29–48.

———. 2007e. The Search for Redemption: Julia Kristeva and Slavoj Žižek on Marx, Psychoanalysis and Religion. *Filozofija i Društvo (Philosophy and Society)* 32 (1): 153–76.

———. 2008. Julia Kristeva, Marx and the Singularity of Paul. In *Marxist Feminist Criticism of the Bible*, ed. R. Boer and J. Økland. Sheffield: Sheffield Phoenix.

———. forthcoming a. The Anomaly of Interpretation. In *Festschrift for Edgar W. Conrad*, ed. J. Kelso, M. Carden, and R. Boer.

———. forthcoming b. *Criticism of Earth: On Marxism and Theology IV*. Leiden: Brill.

———. in press. *Criticism of Religion: On Marxism and Theology II*. Historical Materialism Book Series. Leiden: E. J. Brill.

Bousma, William J. 1988. *John Calvin: A Sixteenth-Century Portrait*. New York: Oxford University Press.

Boyarin, Daniel. 1994. *A Radical Jew: Paul and the Politics of Identity*. Berkeley, CA: University of California Press.

———. 2004. Paul and Genealogy of Gender. In *A Feminist Companion to Paul*. Ed. A.-J. Levine and M. Blickenstaff. London: T&T Clark.

Brettler, Marc. 1994. How the Books of the Hebrew Bible Were Chosen. In *Approaches to the Bible: The Best of Bible Review*. Vol 1, *Composition, Transmission and Language*, ed. H. Minkoff. Washington, DC: Biblical Archaeology Society.

Briggs, Sheila. 2000. Paul on Bondage and Freedom in Imperial Roman Society. In *Paul and Politics: Ekklesia, Israel, Imperium, Interpretation; Essays in Honor of Krister Stendahl*, ed. R. A. Horsley. Harrisburg, PA: Trinity Press International.

Calvin, John. 1844a. *Commentary upon the Acts of the Apostles*. Vol. 1. Trans. C. Fetherstone and H. Beveridge. Edinburgh: Calvin Translation Society.

———. 1844b. *Commentary upon the Epistle of Saint Paul to the Romans*. Trans. C. Rosdell and H. Beveridge. Edinburgh: Calvin Translation Society.

———. 1845. *Commentary on the Book of Psalms*. Vol. 1. Trans. J. Anderson. Edinburgh: Calvin Translation Society.

———. 1846. *Commentaries on the Twelve Minor Prophets: Joel, Amos, Obadiah*. Vol. 2. Trans. J. Owen. Edinburgh: Calvin Translation Society.

———. 1847a. *Commentaries on the First Book of Moses Called Genesis*. Trans. J. King. Edinburgh: Calvin Translation Society.

———. 1847b. *Commentaries on the Twelve Minor Prophets: Jonah, Micah, Nahum*. Vol. 3. Trans. J. Owen. Edinburgh: Calvin Translation Society.

———. 1848. *Commentary on the Epistles of Paul the Apostle to the Corinthians.* Vol. 1. Trans. C. Rosdell and H. Beveridge. Edinburgh: Calvin Translation Society.

———. 1849a. *Commentaries on First Twenty Chapters of the Book of the Prophet Ezekiel.* Vol. 1. Trans. T. Myers. Edinburgh: Calvin Translation Society.

———. 1849b. *Commentaries on the Twelve Minor Prophets.* Vol. 5. Trans. C. Rosdell and H. Beveridge. Edinburgh: Calvin Translation Society.

———. 1849c. *Commentary on the Epistles of Paul the Apostle to the Corinthians.* Vol. 2. Trans. C. Rosdell and H. Beveridge. Edinburgh: Calvin Translation Society.

———. 1850. *Commentary on the Book of the Prophet Isaiah.* Vol. 1. Trans. W. Pringle. Edinburgh: Calvin Translation Society.

———. 1852a. *Commentaries on the Book of the Prophet Daniel.* Vol. 1. Trans. C. Rosdell and H. Beveridge. Edinburgh: Calvin Translation Society.

———. 1852b. *Commentaries on the Last Four Books of Moses Arranged in the Form of a Harmony.* Vol. 1. Trans. C. W. Bingham. Edinburgh: Calvin Translation Society.

———. 1852c. *Commentary on the Book of the Prophet Isaiah.* Vol. 3. Trans. W. Pringle. Edinburgh: Calvin Translation Society.

———. 1853. *Commentary on the Book of the Prophet Isaiah.* Vol. 4. Trans. W. Pringle. Edinburgh: Calvin Translation Society.

———. 1854a. *Commentaries on the Book of the Prophet Jeremiah and the Lamentations.* Vol. 4. Trans. J. Owen. Edinburgh: Calvin Translation Society.

———. 1854b. *Commentaries upon the Epistles of Paul to the Galatians and Ephesians.* Trans. C. Rosdell and H. Beveridge. Edinburgh: Calvin Translation Society.

———. 1855. *Commentaries on the Catholic Epistles.* Trans. J. Owen. Edinburgh: Calvin Translation Society.

———. 1856. *Commentaries on the Epistles to Timothy, Titus, and Philemon.* Trans. W. Pringle. Edinburgh: Calvin Translation Society.

———. 1989. *Institutes of the Christian Religion.* Trans. H. Beveridge. Grand Rapids: Wm. B. Eerdmans Publishing Co.

———. 2006 [1960]. *Institutes of the Christian Religion.* Trans. F. L. Battles. 2 vols. Library of Christian Classics. Louisville, KY: Westminster John Knox Press.

Calvini, Johannes. 1957 [1559]. *Institutiones Christianae religionis.* Ed. P. Barth and G. Niesel. 3 vols, *Opera Selecta.* Munich: Chr. Kaiser.

Carr, David M. 1996. Canonization in the Context of Community. In *A Gift of God in Due Season*, ed. R. D. Weis and D. M. Carr. Sheffield: Sheffield Academic Press.

Chappuis, Jean-Marc. 1987. The Reformation and the Formation of the Person. *The Ecumenical Review* 39:4–22.

Corley, Kathleen E. 2004. Women's Inheritance Rights in Antiquity and Paul's Metaphor of Adoption. In *A Feminist Companion to Paul*, ed. A.-J. Levine and M. Blickenstaff. London: T&T Clark.

Davies, Philip R. 1998. *Scribes and Schools: The Canonization of the Hebrew Scriptures*. Louisville, KY: Westminster John Knox Press.

Debord, Guy. 1995. *Society of the Spectacle*. Trans. D. Nicholson-Smith. London: Zone Books.

Dommen, Edward. 2007. Calvin and the Environment: Calvin's Views Examined through the Prism of Present-Day Concerns, and Especially of Sustainable Development. In *John Calvin Rediscovered: The Impact of His Social and Economic Thought*, ed. E. Dommen and J. B. Bratt. Louisville, KY: Westminster John Knox Press.

Dommen, Edward, and James B. Bratt, eds. 2007. *John Calvin Rediscovered: The Impact of His Social and Economic Thought*. Louisville, KY: Westminster John Knox Press.

Douglass, Jane Dempsey. 1985. *Women, Freedom and Calvin*. Philadelphia: Westminster Press.

du Cros, Rémi Tessier 1999. *Jean Calvin, de la réforme à la révolution*. Paris: L'Harmattan.

Engberg-Pedersen, Troels. 2000. *Paul and the Stoics*. Louisville, KY: Westminster John Knox Press.

Engels, Frederick. 1960 [1850]. Der deutsche Bauernkrieg. In *Karl Marx/ Friedrich Engels—Werke*. Berlin: Dietz.

———. 1975 [1846]. The Condition of the Working-Class in England. In *Marx and Engels Collected Works*. Vol. 4. Moscow: Progress Publishers.

———. 1978 [1850]. The Peasant War in Germany. In *Marx and Engels Collected Works*. Vol. 10. Moscow: Progress Publishers.

———. 1990. On the History of Early Christianity. In *Marx and Engels Collected Works*. Vol. 27. Moscow: Progress Publishers.

Farris, Sara. 2007. *The "Individual" of Social Change. The Anti-Authoritarian Nature of Modernity in Max Weber*. Amsterdam: International Institute for Social History.

Fitzmyer, Joseph A. 2008. *First Corinthians*. Anchor Yale Bible Commentaries. New Haven, CT: Yale University Press.

Foucault, Michel. 1979. *Discipline and Punish: The Birth of the Clinic*. Trans. A. Sheridan. New York: Vintage.

Freud, Sigmund. 2001 [1920]. Beyond the Pleasure Principle. In *The Standard Edition of the Complete Psychological Works of Sigmund Freud*. London: Vintage.

Friedman, Milton. 2002. *Capitalism and Freedom: Fortieth Anniversary Edition*. Chicago: University of Chicago Press.

Glancy, Jennifer A. 2006. *Slavery in Early Christianity*. Minneapolis: Augsburg Fortress.

Goldmann, Lucien. 1959. *Le Dieu caché: Études sur la vision tragiques dans les Pensées de Pascal et dans le théâtre de Racine*. Paris: Éditions Gallimard.

———. 1964. *The Hidden God: A Study of the Tragic Vision the Pensées of Pascal and the Tragedies of Racine*. Trans. P. Thody. New York: Humanities Press.

Graham, W. Fred. 1978. *The Constructive Revolutionary: John Calvin and His Socio-Economic Impact*. Atlanta: John Knox Press.
Gramsci, Antonio. 1996. *Prison Notebooks*. Trans. J. A. Buttigieg. Ed. L. D. Kritzman. Vol. 2, *European Perspectives*. New York: Columbia University Press. Original edition, Quaderni del carcere.
Hamilton, Peter, ed. 1991. *Max Weber, Critical Assessment 1*. London: Routledge.
Hancock, Ralph C. 1989. *Calvin and the Foundations of Modern Politics*. Ithaca, NY: Cornell University Press.
Heidegger, Martin. 2004. *The Phenomenology of Religious Life*. Trans. M. Fritsch and J. A. Gosetti-Ferencei. Bloomington: Indiana University Press.
Helm, Paul. 2004. *John Calvin's Ideas*. Oxford: Oxford University Press.
Hobbes, Thomas. 1962 [1651]. *Leviathan, or the Matter, Forme and Power of a Commonwealth Ecclesiastical and Civil*. New York: Collier Books.
Höpfl, Harro. 1982. *The Christian Polity of John Calvin*. Cambridge: Cambridge University Press.
Horsley, Richard A., ed. 1997. *Paul and Empire: Religion and Power in Roman Imperial Society*. Harrisburg, PA: Trinity Press International.
Howard, Tal. 1993. Charisma and History: The Case of Münster, Westphalia, 1534–1535. *Essays in History* 35:49–64.
Huizinga, Johan. 1924. *The Waning of the Middle Ages: A Study of the Forms of Life, Thought and Art in France and the Netherlands in the XIVth and XVth Centuries*. Trans. F. Hopman. London: E. Arnold & Co.
Jameson, Fredric. 1981. *The Political Unconscious: Narrative as a Socially Symbolic Act*. Ithaca, NY: Cornell University Press.
Kautsky, Karl. 1947 [1895–1897]. *Vorläufer des neueren Sozialismus*. 2 vols. Berlin: J. H. W. Dietz.
———. 2001. *Foundations of Christianity*. Trans. H. F. Mins. http://marxists.org. Original edition, German, 1908. London: Russell & Russell, 1953 (accessed May 5, 2008).
———. 2002 [1897]. *Communism in Central Europe in the Time of the Reformation*. Trans. J. L. Mulliken and E. G. Mulliken. http://www.marxists.org. Original edition, London: Fisher & Unwin, 1897 (accessed May 5, 2008).
Keener, Craig S. 2005. *1–2 Corinthians*. New Cambridge Bible Commentary. Cambridge: Cambridge University Press.
Kelly, Douglas F. 1992. *The Emergence of Liberty in the Modern World: The Influence of Calvin on Five Governments from the 16th through 18th Centuries*. Phillipsburg, NJ: Presbyterian and Reformed Publishing Co.
Kingdon, Robert. 1975. Was the Protestant Reformation a Revolution? The Case of Geneva. In *Church, Society and Politics*, ed. D. Baker. Oxford: Basil Blackwell.
Kristeva, Julia. 1983. *Histoires d'amour*. Paris: Éditions Denoël.
———. 1987. *Tales of Love*. Trans. L. S. Roudiez. New York: Columbia University Press.

———. 1988. *Étrangers à nous-mêmes*. Paris: Gallimard.
———. 1991. *Strangers to Ourselves*. Trans. L. S. Roudiez. New York: Columbia University Press.
Lenin, Vladimir I. 1975. Political Report of the Central Committee of R.C.P.(B.) March 27, 1922. In *Selected Works*. Vol. 3. Moscow: Progress Publishers.
Lévi-Strauss, Claude. 1989. *Tristes tropiques*. Trans. J. Weightman and D. Weightman. London: Pan.
Little, David. 1986. Reformed Faith and Religious Liberty. *Church and Society* 76:5–28.
Longenecker, Richard N. 1990. *Galatians*. Word Biblical Commentary 41. Waco, TX: Word Books.
Löwy, Michael. 1992. *Redemption and Utopia: Jewish Libertarian Thought in Central Europe; A Study in Elective Affinity*. Stanford, CA: Stanford University Press.
Luther, Martin. 1959. *Luther's Works*. Vol. 36, *Word and Sacrament II*, ed. Helmut T. Lehmann and Abdell R. Wentz. Philadelphia: Fortress Press.
Luxemburg, Rosa. 2004. *Socialism and the Churches*. Trans. J. Punto. http://www.marxists.org (accessed March 20, 2008). Original edition, Polish Social Democratic Party, 1905. English Trans. Colombo, Sri Lanka: A Young Socialist Publication, 1972.
Malina, Bruce J., and Jerome H. Neyrey. 1996. *Portraits of Paul: An Archaeology of Ancient Personality*. Louisville, KY: Westminster John Knox Press.
Martin, Dale, B. 1995. *The Corinthian Body*. New Haven, CT: Yale University Press.
———.1999. *The Corinthian Body*. New Haven, CT: Yale University Press.
Martyn, J. Louis. 2004. *Galatians*. Anchor Yale Bible Commentaries. New Haven, CT: Yale University Press.
Marx, Karl. 1975. Contribution to the Critique of Hegel's Philosophy of Law. In *Marx and Engels Collected Works*. Moscow: Progress Publishers.
Matera, Frank J. 2007. *Galatians*. Sacra Pagina 9. Ed. Daniel J. Harrington. Collegeville, MN: Liturgical Press.
McDonald, Lee, and James A. Sanders. 2002. *The Canon Debate*. Peabody, MA: Hendrickson Publishers.
McGrath, Alister E. 1990. *A Life of John Calvin: A Study in the Shaping of Western Culture*. Oxford: Blackwell.
McKim, Donald K., ed. 2006. *Calvin and the Bible*. Cambridge: Cambridge University Press.
McNeill, John T. 1949. The Democratic Element in Calvin's Thought. *Church History* 18:153–71.
Mentzer, Raymond A., and Andrew Spicer, eds. 2002. *Society and Culture in the Huguenot World, 1559–1685*. Cambridge: Cambridge University Press.
Moore, Stephen. 2006. *Empire and Apocalypse: Postcolonialism and the New Testament*. Sheffield: Sheffield Phoenix.

Müntzer, Thomas. 1988. *The Collected Works of Thomas Müntzer*. Trans. P. Matheson. Edinburgh: T&T Clark.
Økland, Jorunn, and Roland Boer. 2008. Towards Marxist Feminist Biblical Criticism. In *Marxist Feminist Criticism of the Bible*, ed. R. Boer and J. Økland. Sheffield: Sheffield Phoenix.
Parkin, Frank. 2003. *Max Weber*. London: Routledge.
Perelman, Michael. 2000. *The Invention of Capitalism: Classical Political Economy and the Secret History of Primitive Accumulation*. Durham, NC: Duke University Press.
Sayer, Derek. 1990. *Capitalism and Modernity: An Excursus on Marx and Weber*. London: Routledge.
Sichère, Bernard. 2003. *Le jour est proche: La révolution selon Paul*. Paris: Desclée de Brouwer.
Skinner, Quentin. 1978. *The Foundations of Modern Political Thought*. Vol. 2, *The Age of Reformation*. Cambridge: Cambridge University Press.
Smith, James A. 2005. *Marks of an Apostle: Deconstruction, Philippians, and Problematizing Pauline Theology*. Atlanta: Society of Biblical Literature.
Sorel, Georges. 1961. *Reflections on Violence*. Trans. T. Hulme and J. Roth. New York: Collier.
Spinoza, Benedict de. 1951 [1670]. *A Theologico-Political Treatise*. Trans. R. H. M. Elwes. New York: Dover.
Sprinker, Michael. 1987. *Imaginary Relations: Aesthetics and Ideology in the Theory of Historical Materialism*. London: Verso.
Steinmetz, David Curtis. 1995. *Calvin in Context*. New York: Oxford University Press.
Stevenson, William R. 1999. *Sovereign Grace: The Place and Significance of Christian Freedom in John Calvin's Political Thought*. New York: Oxford University Press.
———. 2004. Calvin and Political Issues. In *The Cambridge Companion to John Calvin*, ed. D. K. McKim. Cambridge: Cambridge University Press.
Stückelberger, Christoph. 2007. Calvin, Calvinism, and Capitalism: The Challenges of New Interest in Asia. In *John Calvin Rediscovered: The Impact of His Social and Economic Thought*, ed. E. Dommen and J. B. Bratt. Louisville, KY: Westminster John Knox Press.
Sundberg, Albert C. 1964. *The Old Testament of the Early Church: A Study of Canon*. Havard Theological Studies 20. Cambridge, MA: Harvard University Press.
Surin, Kenneth. In press. *Freedom Not Yet: Liberation and the Next World Order*. Durham, NC: Duke University Press.
Swancutt, Diana. 2004. Sexy Stoics and the Reading of Romans 1.18–2.16. In *A Feminist Companion to Paul*, ed. A.-J. Levine and M. Blickenstaff. London: T&T Clark.
Taubes, Jacob. 2004. *The Political Theology of Paul*. Trans. D. Hollander. Cultural Memory in the Present. Stanford, CA: Stanford University Press.

Tawney, R. H. 1926. *Religion and the Rise of Capitalism*. London: Harcourt, Brace & World.
Thistleton, Anthony C. 2000. *The First Epistle to the Corinthians*. New International Greek Testament Commentary. Grand Rapids: Wm. B. Eerdmans Publishing Co.
Thompson, Edward P. 1966. *The Making of the English Working Class*. New York: Vintage.
Thompson, John L. 2004. Calvin as a Biblical Interpreter. In *The Cambridge Companion to John Calvin*, ed. D. K. McKim. Cambridge: Cambridge University Press.
Trigano, Shmuel. 2003. *L'E(xc)lu: Entre Juifs et chrétiens*. Paris: Denoël.
Troeltsch, Ernst. 1992. *The Social Teaching of the Christian Churches*. Louisville, KY: Westminster John Knox Press.
Turner, Bryan S., ed. 1999. *Max Weber: Critical Responses*. London: Routledge.
Turner, Stephen, ed. 2000. *The Cambridge Companion to Weber*. Cambridge: Cambridge University Press.
Van Kley, Dale K. 1999. *The Religious Origins of the French Revolution: From Calvin to the Civil Constitution, 1560–1791*. 2nd ed. New Haven, CT: Yale University Press.
Voegelin, Eric. 1952. *The New Science of Politics*. Chicago: University of Chicago Press.
von Hayek, Friedrich. 1960. *The Constitution of Liberty*. Chicago: University of Chicago Press.
Walzer, Michael. 1965. *The Revolution of the Saints: A Study in the Origins of Radical Politics*. Cambridge, MA: Harvard University Press.
Weber, Max. 1952. *Ancient Judaism*. Trans. D. Martindale. Chicago: Free Press.
Willis-Watkins, David. 1989. Calvin's Prophetic Reinterpretation of Kingship. In *Probing the Reformed Tradition*, ed. E. McKee and B. Armstrong. Louisville, KY: Westminster John Knox Press.
Yinger, Milton A. 1980. *Religion in the Struggle for Power: A Study in the Sociological Study of Religion*. Manchester, NH: Ayer Publishing.
Žižek, Slavoj. 1999. *The Ticklish Subject: The Absent Centre of Political Ontology*. London: Verso.
———. 2001. *On Belief*. London: Routledge.
———. 2003. *The Puppet and the Dwarf: The Perverse Core of Christianity*. Cambridge, MA: MIT.
Žižek, Slavoj and John Milbank. 2009. *The Mostrosity of Christ: Paradox or Dialectic?* Cambridge, MA: MIT.
Žižek, Slavoj, Eric L. Santner, and Kenneth Reinhard. 2006. *The Neighbor: Three Inquiries in Political Theology*. Chicago: University of Chicago Press.

Scripture Index

OLD TESTAMENT

Exodus
5:1	119
18:13–27	86

Leviticus
11	15n7

1 Samuel
8:11–17	86
24	86

Esther 23

Psalms 43
2	15n7
2:10–11	83, 83n4, 88

Song of Songs 23

Isaiah 35, 37, 119n2
3:14–15	118
10:1–2	83, 83n4, 88
45:1	84
61:1–2	121, 121n3

Jeremiah
32:39–40	42

Ezekiel 113
11:9–20	46n2
11:19	42
36:26	40, 44
36:26–27	45–46

Daniel 17
2:44	15
6:22	92

Amos 37
2:6–7	117, 118n1, 121n3
8:4–6	118, 118n1, 121n3

Micah 37
6:8	120

NEW TESTAMENT

Matthew
3	15n7
25:35–36	119

Mark
10:25	119

Luke 35
1:52	3
4:18–19	121

Acts 35, 37
2:44–45	9, 119
4:32–35	9, 119–20
5:29	92
10:9–16	37

Romans 48–49, 51, 100
1:17	97
2:8–10	97
2:11–29	100
3:9	97
3:10–18	41
3:13	41
3:15	41
3:21–22	97
3:31	99
4	97, 102
5–6	97
5:11–13	97
5:16–18	97
5:20–21	97
5:21	97
6	97
6:1	97, 99
6:9–11	97
6:14	49
6:14–15	97, 98
6:15	99
6:23	97
7	97, 101
7:4	97
7:6	99
7:10	97
7:11	99
7:16	99
7:25	97
8:2	97, 102
8:6	97
8:9–10	97
8:29–30	103
8:38	97
9–11	100
9:11	97
9:13	97
9:24	97
10:4	97
10:6	97
10:12	97
11:6	97
11:7	97
11:28	97
13	110
13:1	99
13:1–2	81
13:14	97
14:1	63
14:13	63
14:14	62
15:1	63

1 Corinthians	99, 100	Galatians	62, 70, 99, 100	Philippians	
1:23	97	2	97, 101	1:20	97
6:16	96, 97	2:11–16	100	3:1–4	97
7:20	99	2:16	97	3:9	97
7:20–22	97, 101	2:17	97	Colossians	35
7:23	92, 129	2:21	97		
8:9	63	3:1	97	1 Timothy	35
8:12	97	3:10	99	2:1–2	81, 81n2
9:21	97	3:11	97	6:16	33
10:25	63	3:13	97	2 Timothy	35
10:29	63	3:22	97		
10:32	63	3:24	97	Titus	
12:13	97	3:28	97, 98, 99, 101	3:1	81, 81n2
15:3	97	5:4	97	Hebrews	23
15:17	97	5:5	97		
15:22	97	5:13	63	1 Peter	
15:39	97	5:14	97	2:13	81, 81n2
15:50	97	6:2	97	Revelation	17
		6:13	97		
2 Corinthians	99	Ephesians	35		
2:16	97	2:20	25		
4:10–12	97	6:1	90		
5:19	97				

Subject Index

Abraham, 102
absolute power, 5n1, 79–80
Adam, 97, 102, 103, 115
Affaire des Placards, 6–9, 13, 58, 70, 112
Agamben, Giorgio, xx
Aichele, George, 23n2, 95–96
Allen, J. W. A., xxiin7
Althusser, Louis, 104
Anabaptists, 9–13, 18, 19, 34, 66, 99, 104, 120
anarchy, 78–80, 81, 114
Anderson, Perry, 5n1, 108
anthropocentrism, 124–25
Antichrist, xxvii
Apostasy Act, 60–61
Aretino, 66
aristocracy of salvation, 52–55, 113, 123
Astruc, Jean, 34
Augustine, xi, xxv, 24, 34, 66–67
Australia, ix–x, 8, 35–36, 52–53, 66, 71–72, 122
auto-faith, 25–27, 31, 113

Badiou, Alain, xx
Barth, P., xii
Battles, Ford Lewis, xii
Bendix, Reinhard, xixn4
Benedict, Philip, 6n2
Berthoud, Garielle, 7n4
Beukelszoon, Jan, 11, 12
Beveridge, Henry, xii, 26
Bible
   age, reliability, and pedigree of, 29n4
   allegorical interpretation of, 95
   authors of, 25, 31, 34, 35
   as auto-faith document, 25–27, 31, 113
   Calvin's commentaries on, 96, 96n4

Calvin's high view of, xv, 21, 32–37, 33n6, 96, 112–13, 115, 116–17, 121
Calvin's reading of, 93–97, 99–104, 115
canon of, 23, 23n2, 34
chicken-and-egg argument on, 25, 31
Church's interpretation of, 22–24
on communal or communist living, 119–21
conservative position on, 32–36
diagram of, 30–32
on economic injustice and oppression, 37, 117–19
guidance for understanding, 37
historical-critical approach to, 34–35, 95
and Holy Spirit, 23, 26, 28–32, 113
inerrancy of, 35
Institutes texts on, 22, 25, 26
mouth-of-God argument on, 27–28, 33–34, 36–37, 113, 117
multivocality of, xvi, 70, 94–97, 115
as out of reach of human hands, 22–24, 112–13
radical position on, 36–37, 116–21
self-sufficiency of, 25–27
tensions and contradictions in, 93–94
witness-of-the-Holy-Spirit position on, 28–30, 31
See also Paul
Biéler, Andre, xviin3, xxii
Blanton, Ward, xx
blasphemy, 61, 77
Bloch, Ernst, 17, 95
Boeckbinder, Bartholomeus, 11, 12
Boer, Roland
   personal reflections by, ix–x, 8, 35–36, 52–53, 66, 71–72, 94
   writings by, xxi–xxii, 35n8, 95, 97n5, 108, 124n4, 127, 131

143

SUBJECT INDEX

Bousma, William J., xxiii, xxiv, 75n1
Boyarin, Daniel, 107n10
Bratt, James B., xviin3
Brettler, Marc, 23n2
Briggs, Sheila, 108n11

Caesar Augustus, 107
calamities, xxvi
Calvin, John
 compared with Paul, xvi–xvii
 context of, compared with Paul, xvi–xvii, 104–10, 115–16
 context of study of, xviii–xxiv
 death of, x
 economic and social ramifications of theology of, 106, 115
 health problems of, x–xi
 organization and order in writings by, 50–52, 72–73
 as revolutionary, xxii–xxiii, 1–6, 18–20, 111–16
 sentence production of, xxiv–xxvii
 structural tensions in thought of, xxiii–xxiv
 tension between radical and conservative elements in, xv–xviii, 20, 93, 111–16
 theological tensions in writings by, xvn1
 writings by, xi
 See also Bible; freedom; grace; politics
capitalism, xix, 93, 105–6, 115, 122, 125, 126
Carr, David M., 23n2
charisma, 55
Chaucer, Geoffrey, 95
chicken-and-egg argument on the Bible, 25, 31
Christ. *See* Jesus Christ
Christian freedom. *See* freedom
Churchill, Winston, 50–51
civil disobedience, xvi, 76–77, 87–92, 114–15, 129–31
civil government. *See* politics
communal or communist living, 119–21
confession, 73n5
Constantine, 23, 110
conversion/revolution, 44–45
Corley, Kathleen E., 107n10
corruption, 40–42, 43, 47. *See also* sin
Cuyper, Wilhelm de, 12
Cyrus, king of Medes and Persians, 84

David, 86
Davies, Philip R., 23n2
death, 102–3, 107, 109, 115
Debord, Guy, xvin2
democracy, 126
democracy of depravity, 41–42, 53–55, 83, 101, 103, 113, 122–23. *See also* sin
Denmark, 60
De Vries, Hent, xx
disobedience. *See* obedience
Dommen, Edward, xvin2, xviin3
Donatists, 34
Douglass, Jane Dempsey, 62n3
du Cros, Rémi Tessier, xixn4, xxii, 62

ecology, xvin2
Ehud, 84
ekklesia, xx, 110
enclosure movements, 105
Engberg-Pedersen, Troels, 107n10
Engels, Friedrich, 13, 16–17, 106, 120
England, 60–61, 105, 106
Erasmus, 72
Esther, 84
evil, 40–42, 43, 47

faith
 Bible as auto-faith document, 25–27, 31, 113
 and conversion/revolution, 44–45
 freedom in practice of, 59, 62–64, 72, 114, 125
 as gift from God, 24, 40
 and grace, 40, 42–44, 113
 justification by faith, 49, 100–102, 106, 123
 Paul on, 97, 98, 107, 109
Farris, Sara, xixn4
feudalism, 1–6, 93, 105, 106, 115, 125
Fitzmyer, Joseph A., 98n7
Ford, Henry, xviii
Foucault, Michel, 67
Francis I, king of France, 1–2, 4, 7–8, 12, 17, 18–20, 78, 90, 99, 112
freedom
 current meanings of term, 126–28
 curtailing of, 59–64, 73
 and democracy, 126
 formal versus actual freedom, 128

in Homer's *Odyssey*, 57–58
Institutes texts on, 59–60, 62, 64, 68–69
from law and freedom for Christ, 59, 63, 72, 73, 114, 125
Lenin on, 128
and liberation, 127–28
necessity of, 58
to obey God's will, 59, 60–64, 72, 73, 114, 125
paradox of Calvinist legalism, 70–73
personal and individual freedom, 126–27
in practice of the faith, 59, 62–64, 72, 114, 125
private-public distinction on, xvi, 64–70, 73, 114, 125–26
radical position on, 116, 125–29
types of, xvi, 58–64, 72–73, 113–14, 125
Freud, Sigmund, 69–70, 105
Friedman, Milton, 126

Gentiles and Jews, 97, 98, 100–101, 103, 107, 109, 115
Gideon, 84
Glancy, Jennifer, 108n11
God
  and agents for punishment of rulers, 82–85, 88, 114, 129–31
  claims of having God on their side, 130–31
  and corruption of human beings, 41–42, 43, 47
  mouth-of-God argument on Bible, 27–28, 33–34, 36–37, 113, 117
  obedience to, 59, 60–64, 75–76, 90–91, 112, 114, 115, 125, 129
  self-sufficiency of, 27
  Trinitarian nature of, 32
  wrath of, against rulers, 83, 90
  See also Holy Spirit; Jesus Christ
Goldmann, Lucien, 124n4
government. *See* politics
grace
  control of, 48–55
  and corruption, 40–42, 43, 47
  and faith, 40, 42–44, 113
  and heart of flesh, 45–48, 113
  Institutes texts on, 40, 41, 43–46, 49, 52, 54

neatly ordered grace, 48–52
Paul on, xvi, 97, 98, 99, 107, 109
and predestination, 52–55, 113
radical position on, xvi, 39–48, 116, 122–25
and reconciliation and sanctification, 49, 51–52
revolutionary paradox of, 55–56
and salvation, 24, 39, 113
and will, 42–44
Graham, W. Fred, xvii, xixn4, xxiii, xxiv, 77
Gramsci, Antonio, xxiv
Gunn, David, 49n3

Haman, 84
Hamilton, Peter, xixn4
Hancock, Ralph C., xixn4, xxii, xxiin7
heart of flesh, 45–48, 113. *See also* grace
Heidegger, Martin, xx
Helm, Paul, 24n3
hierarchy, 1–6, 46–47
Hobbes, Thomas, 34
Hoffman, Melchior, 10
Holy Spirit
  and Bible, 23, 26, 28–32, 113
  and Christ, 33
  and sanctification, 51
Homer, 57–58
Höpfl, Harro, xvii, xxiin7
Horsley, Richard, 107–8
Howard, Tal, 12
Huizinga, Johan, 10

idolatry, xvin2, 77, 98
imaginary resolution, 104–5
Institutes of the Christian Religion (Calvin)
  as guide to the Bible, 37
  sentence style of, xxiv–xxvii
  tension between radical and conservative elements in, xv–xviii
  translations of, xi–xii, 49n3
  See also Bible; freedom; grace; politics
Islam, xviii

Jameson, Fredric, 104
Jansenism, 124n4
Jesus Christ
  and Adam, 97, 102, 103, 115
  and Calvin's high view of Bible, 32–33

Jesus Christ (*continued*)
  on communal living, 121
  death and resurrection of, 102, 106, 109
  on economic injustice and oppression, 37, 117, 119
  freedom from law and freedom for, 59, 63, 70, 72, 73, 114, 125
  and grace, 49–52
  and Holy Spirit, 33
  Paul on, 97–99
Jews and Gentiles, 97, 98, 100–101, 103, 107, 109, 115
John Chrysostom, xxv
Joyce, James, 95
Judaism, xxn5. *See also* Jews and Gentiles
justification by faith, 49, 100–102, 106, 123
justification by works, 103, 106, 123

Kautsky, Karl, 16–17, 120
Keener, Craig S., 98n7
Kelly, Douglas F., xxii
Kierkegaard, Søren, xi
Kingdon, Robert, xxii
Kristeva, Julia, xx–xxi

law
  basis of, 81
  freedom from law and freedom for Christ, 59, 63, 72, 73, 114, 125
  Paul on, 97–99, 101–2, 107, 109
  spiritual and temporal laws, 80–81
  See also politics
Lazarus, 10
Lenin, V. I., 128
Lévi-Strauss, Claude, 104, 105
liberalism, 61–62
liberation, 127–28. *See also* freedom
liberation theology, 127, 128
liberty. *See* freedom
libido, 65
Life of Brian, The, 9n5
Little, David, xxiii
Longenecker, Richard N., 98n7
Lord's Supper, 7
Löwy, Michael, xxn5
Luther, Martin, xix, 14–18, 67, 72, 82, 120, 123
Luxemburg, Rosa, 120

magistrates, 85–88, 91, 114
Malina, Bruce J., 107n10
Manicheans, 34
Marcourt, Antoine de, 7n4
Marguerite de Navarre, 7
Martin, Dale B., 98n7, 107n10
Martyn, J. Louis, 98n7
Marx, Karl, xi, xxiv, 13, 67
Matera, Frank J., 98n7
Matheson, Peter, 15n6
Matthys, Jan, 10, 11, 12
McDonald, Lee, 23n2
McGrath, Alistair E., xixn4
McKim, Donald K., 94n1
McNeill, John T., xxii
Melanchthon, Philipp, 5n1
Metzger, Raymond A., 6n2
Milbank, John, xx
Milon, Barthélemi, 8
Moab, 84
modes of production, 104, 105–6
monarchy
  absolute monarchs, 5n1
  and magistrates, 85–88, 91, 114
  and medieval feudal society, 1–6
  symbol of power of, 4
  See also politics
monasteries, xxvi–xxvii, 120
Moore, Stephen, 110
Mordecai, 84
Moses, 3, 17, 34, 35, 81, 84, 117, 119
mouth-of-God argument on the Bible, 27–28, 33–34, 36–37, 113, 117
Münster Revolution, 9–13, 58, 66, 70, 112, 113
Müntzer, Thomas, 14–18, 66, 83

Netherlands, ix–x, 12
Neyrey, Jerome H., 107n10
Niesel, G., xii
Noah, 50, 52
Norway, 127

obedience
  and disobedience against tyrannical rulers, xvi, 76–77, 87–92, 114–15, 129–31
  to God, 59, 60–64, 75–76, 90–91, 112, 114, 115, 125, 129

to parents, 90n5
to rulers, 75–76, 81–82, 82n3, 85, 87–89, 90n5, 114
Odyssey (Homer), 57–58
Økland, Jorunn, 127
Opera Selecta (Calvin), xii
opinion versus truth, 24
original sin, 40–42
Othniel, 84

Parkin, Frank, xixn4
Paul
  Boer on, 97n5
  Calvin's reading of, 99–104, 115
  context of, compared with Calvin, xvi–xvii, 104–10, 107n10, 115–16
  contradictions and oppositions in, 97–99, 107–10, 115
  and *ekklesia*, xx, 110
  on faith, 97, 98, 107, 109
  on grace, xvi, 97, 98, 99, 107, 109
  on law, 97–99, 101–2, 107, 109
  letters by, 35
  political nature of letters of, xx–xxi
  and Roman Empire, 110
  on sin, 97, 99, 109, 115
  socioeconomic tension and tumult during time of, 107–9, 107n10
  tension between radical and conservative elements in, xvi, 109–10, 115–16
pax Romana, 107–8
Peasants' Revolt, 10, 13–18, 58, 70, 105, 112
Pelagianism, 34, 72
Pelagius, xxv
Perelman, Michael, 105–6
Peter, 37, 92
Placards Affair, 6–9, 13, 58, 70, 112
Plato, 24
political theology, xx–xxi
politics
  and absolute power, 5n1, 79–80
  aristocratic government with popular elements, 80
  basis of law, 81
  and disobedience against tyrannical rulers, xvi, 76–77, 87–92, 114–15, 129–31

and God and agents for punishment of rulers, 82–85, 88, 114, 129–31
Institutes texts on, 75–76, 75n1, 82, 83, 88–90
and magistrates, 85–88, 91, 114
obedience to rulers, 75–76, 81–82, 82n3, 87–89, 90n5, 114
radical position on, 116, 129–31
spiritual and temporal laws, 80–81
and temporal-spiritual tension, 76–78
and tension between anarchy and tyranny, 78–80, 81, 114
and ungodly ruler, 80–88
predestination, 52–55, 113, 123–24

reconciliation, 49, 51–52
Reinhard, Kenneth, xx
revolution
  Calvin as revolutionary, xxii–xxiii, 1–6, 18–20, 111–16
  definition of, 3–4
  examples of, 48, 56
  faith and conversion/revolution, 44–45
  and Müntzer, 13–18
  paradox of, 55–56, 113
  and radical Bible, 36–37, 116–21
  and radical freedom, 116, 125–29
  and radical grace, xvi, 39–48, 116, 122–25
  and radical position on politics, 116, 129–31
revolutionary paradox, 55–56, 113
Roman Catholic Church
  Calvin's attacks on, xxvi–xxvii
  and canon of Bible, 23, 23n2, 34
  and monasteries, xxvi–xxvii, 120
  and Münster Revolution, 9–13
  and Placards Affair, 6–9, 13, 58, 70, 112
  and transubstantiation, 7
Roman Empire, 107–8, 107n10, 110
Rothmann, Bernhard, 11
rulership. *See* monarchy; politics

Sacred Economy, 108, 110, 115
salvation, 24, 39, 49–50, 52–55, 101, 102n9, 113
sanctification, 49, 51, 52, 103
Sanders, James A., 23n2

Santner, Eric L., xx
Saul, 86
Sayer, Derek, xixn4
Scripture. *See* Bible
Shakespeare, William, 95
Shepherd of Hermes, The, 23
Sichère, Bernard, xx
sin
  and death, 102–3
  and democracy of depravity, 41–42,
    53–55, 83, 101, 103, 113, 122–23
  and grace, 40–42, 43, 47, 51–52
  against Holy Spirit, 71
  of missing church on Sunday, 71
  original sin, 40–42
  Paul on, 97, 99, 109, 115
  of rulers, 83, 129
Skinner, Quentin, 6n2
slaves, 97, 98, 101, 107–10, 115, 118, 125
sleep, 60n2
Smith, James A., 107n10
Sorel, Georges, xxiv
Spicer, Andrew, 6n2
Spinoza, Benedict de, 34
spiritual escapism, 79
Sprinker, Michael, 104
Steinmetz, David Curtis, 75n1
Stevenson, William R., xvii, xxiii, 62,
  73n5, 75n1, 81n2
Stoics, 107n10
Stückelberger, Christoph, xixn4
Sunday observance, 61, 71–72
Sundberg, Albert C., 23n2
Surin, Kenneth, 126
Swancutt, Diana, 107n10
Sweden, 60

Taubes, Jacob, xx
Tawney, R. H., xixn4, xxii–xxiii, 61

Taylorization, xviii, xxi
Ten Commandments, 73n5, 90n5
theological suspicion, 131
Thistleton, Anthony, 98n7
Thomas Aquinas, 50
Thompson, E. P., 106
Thompson, J., 96n2
transubstantiation, 7
Trigano, Shmuel, xx
Trinitarian relationship, 32. *See also* God;
  Holy Spirit; Jesus Christ
Troeltsch, Ernst, 55
truth versus opinion, 24
Turner, Bryan, xixn4
Turner, Stephen, xixn4
tyranny, xvi, 76–80, 81, 87–92, 114–15,
  129–31

unhappiness, xxvi

Van Kley, Dale K., xviin3
Voegelin, Eric, xxiii
Voltaire, x
von Hayek, Friedrich, 126

Waldeck, Franz von, 11
Walzer, Michael, xxiii
Wassenberger Prädikanten, 11
Watson, Frances, 35n8
Weber, Max, xix–xx, xxii, 106
Wesley, John, 123
will, 42–44
Willis-Watkins, David, 75n1
witness-of-the-Holy-Spirit position on the
  Bible, 28–30, 31

Yinger, Milton A., xixn4

Žižek, Slavoj, xx, 128

www.ingramcontent.com/pod-product-compliance
Lightning Source LLC
Chambersburg PA
CBHW031418290426
44110CB00011B/442